SHOOT
POOL

SHOOT POOL

IAN PANNELL

CHARTWELL
BOOKS, INC.

A QUINTET BOOK

Published by Chartwell Books
A Division of Book Sales, Inc.
110 Enterprise Avenue
Secaucus, New Jersey 07094

ISBN 1-55521-413-4

Reprinted 1993

This book was designed and produced by
Quintet Publishing Limited
6 Blundell Street
London N7 9BH

Creative Director: Peter Bridgewater
Art Director: Ian Hunt
Designer: James Lawrence
Project Editor: Shaun Barrington
Editor: Beverley LeBlanc
Photographer: Paul Forrester

Typeset in Great Britain by
Central Southern Typesetters, Eastbourne
Manufactured in Hong Kong by
Regent Publishing Services Limited
Printed in Hong Kong

Contents

Introduction

Probably more than 50 million people all over the world play pool regularly: but where did this, the most popular of all table games, originate? And who were the great players who popularized it?

The greatest international table game

Pool – or American pocket billiards – is without doubt the most popular international table game played. Since its beginnings before the turn of the century, pool has grown dramatically, and is now played in almost every country of the world. In the US alone, some 30 million people shoot pool. Add to that the 9 million players in Japan and the 7 million British players and you begin to appreciate just how widespread the game is.

As the game has spread, some of the rules of play have been modified in different countries, as well as table and pocket sizes and the sizes and colors of balls. Despite these differences, pool everywhere retains its essential attractions: as a game bridging all cultural, social or economic barriers; and as a game that provides enjoyment and satisfaction to players of vastly different levels of ability.

To the casual observer, pool may appear as a game played by the "boys" in the saloon, with seemingly few rules and not much more skill. Pool is, however, as finely structured as any other table game, demanding great concentration and skill. It is played on a table rarely larger than 9 × 4½ft, the strategy of every game being played out within a cue's length.

The game essentially consists of the controlled movement of 16 balls, a white cue ball and 15 object balls numbered 1–15 in opposing stripes or spots. The game starts with the white ball being played from behind the head string line to split the stack of balls. Each player then plays in turn, leaving the table when he or she makes a mistake, or cannot progress. The player who pots the most balls, or pots the last ball, wins. A simple game with an even simpler objective? Ask any pool player or, if you are lucky, watch the indomitable world champion, American Jim Rempe, raise the game to incredible heights of skill, strategy and gamesmanship. It is to these skills *Shoot Pool* is addressed.

As an individual's standard of play improves, the need to have a competitive edge grows. No player, especially the young of either sex, however gifted, can learn the basic skills of shooting pool just by match play. Bad playing habits are hard to overcome. Without professional guidance these faults lead to games full of mistakes, miscues and mediocrity.

Mediocrity is the greatest sin, as untutored play can often lead to undisciplined behavior at the table. Nothing is worse than a poor game played badly. From the basic stance, through cuing and shot selection, this guide will enable aspiring players to upgrade their game. It will also show the beginner how to play and, with practice, astound his opponent in his first real game, as well as help to hone the skills of the more experienced player.

The rules of pool are not discussed in *Shoot Pool* in any great depth for many reasons. Primarily *Shoot Pool* cannot comment on the accepted rules of play, because they vary from country to country and club to club, and are being continuously amended by numerous different committees.

Only the basic, unchanging rules concern *Shoot Pool*. Learn these by heart and know them well; they form the basis from which your lcoal rules are drawn. A knowledge and understanding of these rules can often be used as a second opponent against any unwary player.

Finally, remember behind the skills of every great player lies a great amount of practice.

The greatest pool players

With such an enormous array of past and present champion pool players it is impossible to mention them all; the list would outweigh the rest of *Shoot Pool* and would end up reading like the book in the Hall of Fame!

We have to be content with reviewing the players without whom pool, or American pocket billiards, would never have left the dark and dingy

One of the most famous – you could say notorious – pool players in history, Minnesota Fats. Willie Mosconi, who had some tremendous battles with Fats at the table, has openly described him as a hustler.

backrooms where it was first played.

The first real champion of pool was the great Ralph Greenleaf. He died at just 51 years but during his life was the 14.1 champion 19 times. His best recorded 14.1 record is a high run of 126 with a high single average of 11.2 in Detroit in 1929. He also took pool to the theater with his trick shot program. Assisted by his attractive wife Nai Tai Tai and an enormous overhead mirror to help spectators have a better view of the play, Greenleaf toured vaudeville throughout the 1920s and 1930s.

Willie Mosconi is the second great name in pool. Born in Philadelphia in 1913, by the age of seven he was displaying the cue talents that, as Greenleaf forecast when he saw him play, would eventually lead the boy to become world cham-

pion. Mosconi was only 20 when Greenleaf took him on a tough 112-day tour during which he managed to win 50 out of the 170 games with Greenleaf.

Mosconi's pool play reached a pitch of perfection in 1940 after a series of tournaments over 6 months, during which he played 224 games and scored 50 runs of 100 or more. His 14.1 record is hard to match: In 1945 he played Arthur Cranfield and in a single match game had a best high run of 127. In Chicago in 1950, playing George Chenier, Mosconi's best game over two innings averaged 18.34. At the 1954 San Francisco world championship match against Luther Lassiter, his best innings during an exhibition match over two games produced a run of 526 . . . and took 3 hours.

Today, Jim Rempe is as popular throughout the

Willie Mosconi won the first of his many world titles in 1941, and was practically unchallenged throughout most of the 1950s. His crown passed to Luther Lassiter and Arthur Cranfield Jr, who dominated in the 1960s.

world as he is in the US and his match record justifies the fame.

Pool attracts the record makers as well. Michael Eufemia of Brooklyn holds the world's record for the longest consecutive high run of 625 made in Logan's Billiard Academy on February 2, 1960. Ross McInnes "the flying Scotsman" holds the world speed pool record by pocketing all 16 balls in just 40.06 seconds. Other players also deserving mention include Richie Florence, winner of the first Lite Beer World Series, and 24-year-old Earl Strickland, named player of the year in 1983. Eddie Charlton has done much to promote pool in Australia. In Europe, Joe Barbara, the British champion, is outstanding.

To omit women pool players would be unforgivable. Players like Dorothy Wise, who first won the women's division of the US Open Pocket Billiards Championship in 1967, have fought for recognition against male prejudice for many years. She plays alongside a notable group of players, including Sheila Bohm, San Lynn Merrick and Geraldine Titcomb.

The origins of pool

Where pool originated from often seems to be a matter of open speculation; every pool player seems to favor a different version. Some like to think the game originated in the deep south, with freed slaves emulating their old masters' game of hazards. Others see its origins in the speak-easy days of prohibition.

The truth is actually more interesting than the myths. Pool has its roots in billiards, a favorite game of the Spanish explorer Capt. Ferdinando de Soto, who landed on the Florida coast in 1539 and introduced the game a year later. More proof of the antiquity of billiards comes from Virginia, where as far back as 1607, the English Cavaliers, escaping from the wrath of Cromwell, found settling down at night easier after a frame or two, as did the French Huguenots who settled in South Carolina about 1690. The game persevered in its original form even after the War of Independence, when it was still being played on tables imported by British army officers.

Some purists maintain billiards is even older, with the game first documented by the French in 1350. Shakespeare even mentions it in the opening scenes of *Anthony and Cleopatra* (Act 2, scene 5) when Charmain is asked by Cleopatra if he would like a game. (He complained of a sore arm and cried off, leaving the honors to Mardian). Even Napoleon played the game after he was imprisoned in St. Helena by the British.

The tables of the 1800s were primitive by today's standards. The bed was made from oak and covered in a coarse baize. The banks fared no better and were made from a woolen list. The balls were generally turned from ivory and rarely matched in size or weight. The most popular game played was English hazards, but all was soon to change.

Edwin Kentfield, an Englishman from Brighton, and the American industrialist John Thurston designed a slate bed table with banks (albeit rudimentary) made from flannel stuffed with cotton waste. This new table was first used about 1827 and upgraded by replacing the banks with the new rubber type in 1845.

Thurston was also responsible for the development and introduction of the first composition balls. The cost of the ivory type was making the game almost exclusively a sport of the very well-off. By 1894, the new Bonzoline composition balls were in play. And not too soon either, as by then some 20,000 elephants were slaughtered annually to feed the demand for ivory billiard balls.

The cue changed as well. Originally called a mace, the craftsmanship of the wood turners converted it to a cue. The last real development of the cue was the addition of a leather tip invented by the French player Mingaud. John Carr, an Englishman from Bath, realized the potential of the new tip by chalking it and was soon providing spectators with his incredible display of English and draw . . . and providing other players, and at some cost to them, Carr's "magical screwing chalk."

American pocket billiards appears to have developed from early forms of snooker, that had its origins in India. It was a hybrid game based on billiards, pyramids and black pool. Snooker was first played in Jubbulpore about 1875 with 15 red balls and six other colored balls. With all these innovations, the game soon spread to Britain and Europe and then across the Atlantic to the billiard halls of the US. The craze for billiards spread to the smaller saloons, and, because of the limited floor space available, the table was shortened from 12 × 6ft to 10 × 5ft. The new composition balls were far less expensive and more readily available than the older ivory sort, and snooker soon replaced billiards on the small tables. Because of the limitation of the smaller table, the six colored balls were soon left out of play, leaving 15 balls in a pyramid. This game was faster still but retained the essence of snooker, playing to the pocket being the primary aim. The need to develop this crude game came when players would call a particular ball, eventually nominating the pocket it was to be played to.

Perhaps even the name "pool" owes its origins to the earlier Indian game of "black pool." None of this is certain, but the American pocket billiards became a real game in 1890 when it was formalized and the balls given the numbers, spots and stripes they still bear. Despite its rather gray beginnings, however, pool today cannot be overshadowed by any other game, billiards, snooker or even carom.

LEFT *The boys in the back room having fun; this early image of pool as a seamy, down-market diversion for wild boys took a long, long time to shake off.*

RIGHT AND BELOW *Pool is as much a part of the American inheritance as jukeboxes and hotdogs, as its continual appearance in the movies attests. Paul Newman's 'The Hustler' was a magnificent exploration of romantic desperation and nobility, with pool as its backdrop.*

OPPOSITE *Some of the top pool players on today's circuit, as illustrated by the twins, bottom right (see page 124).*
1 Earl Strickland 2 Efren Reyes 3 Wade Crane
4 Buddy Hall 5 Steve Mizerak 6 Ray Martin
7 Jimmy Rempe 8 Grady Mathews 9 Lou Butera
10 Danny Diliberto 11 David Howard 12 Mike Massey
13 Mike Sigel 14 Larry Lisciotti.

"THE TWINS" ARTIST
TOM ~ DAN BIRKBECK
1986

The European scene

Many pool players, especially in Britain, maintain pool was first played in London as a shortened version of snooker, using only the 15 balls of the stack and ignoring the other 6 colors. This claim seems to have some credibility, and to substantiate it, four English pool players attempted to play the game using first the standard snooker balls and then a spot and stripe set of pool balls.

The sheer size of the snooker table was the undoing of the game. Although it had some of the essence of pool, the game soon became very boring; once the pack was split, the object balls disappeared into the far flung corners of the table. Straight shots played diagonally across the table required perfect aim and pace – not to mention perfect eyesight as well! – to travel accurately the 16ft from corner to pocket. Could this have been one of the reasons why pool never became popular in the early days? The four players were quite certain, after a game lasting almost an hour, this was indeed the reason!

It was not until the early 1960s pool re-entered Britain. Pool had spread from the US to Australia where it quickly became very popular in the bars and hotels. British amusement machine operators were aware of this new and interesting game and decided to introduce pool into the British bars.

Pool was an immediate success in the venues large enough to accommodate the American tables but the size of these tables excluded the game from many small English pubs. The table manufacturers were quick to identify this demand for a smaller table, the hallmark of today's game.

But all was not well. The pool players were not happy with the first hybrid tables. They still sported the 2¼-inch diameter American balls, and the pockets were so large they seemed to take up all of the available rail left.

A new table with a smaller ball and pocket was designed. With this new table, pool was to become the most widespread table sport in Europe.

While the prize money may not be as great in Europe as it is in the US, there are several major tournaments every year, well organized and well attended.

TOURNAMENT: BLACKPOOL, ENGLAND

THE EUROPEAN GAME

The limitation of the number of tables in any venue (normally only one table) is the reason why 8-ball pool is the predominant version played in Europe. Each game can be a match in itself. To win, a player does not have to amount a certain number of points; instead victory is by pocketing the 8-ball. The usual 14.1 game took too long to resolve, especially when other players were lining up to play, and quicker 8.1 became the normal game played. The first rules were in the pure American style, but these did not suit the game on smaller tables, especially because the tables were coin operated. On these tables, only the cue ball was (and is) returned after being accidentally

A difficult bridge in one of the many pool halls in London. Many players are reluctant to use the rest, and will do so only as a last resort – sometimes to their cost.

pocketed, and the rules were amended to suit this new restriction. BAPTO (the British Association of Pool Table Operators) produced the first nationally accepted rules and started organizing local and area tournaments.

The next step was taken by pool players. The Scottish Pool Association was formed, closely followed by similar associations in Ireland, Wales and England. The first international match played between the newly formed associations was held at Carlisle, England, in March, 1975, and was won by the English team. As the popularity of pool grew throughout the UK, and more and more venues featured pool, the competition to represent leagues, counties and eventually the individual countries blossomed.

These associations produced their own rules and confusion grew from the slight, but vital, differences that arose. After years of futile arguments, sense has prevailed and one set of rules is accepted throughout Europe.

EUROPEAN 8-BALL

The roots of European 8-ball lay in the small one-table venues. The tables are generally 6 × 3ft with the balk line drawn and the foot-spot marked. Usually the spots and stripes are replaced with yellow and red balls; only the 8-ball retains the familiar white spot out of black. The balls are smaller diameter and the pockets much smaller than their American cousins, and the cue ball even smaller.

The rules are drawn as carefully as the game has to be played, and even a casual game can take on the importance of an international match! Beware of the European player who asks for a friendly game ... he is as friendly as Paul Newman in *The Hustler!*

To take a European on at *his* game will need all the expertise you have gained from long practice sessions. You will have to get used to the smaller and more intimate table. Be sure to read and understand the rules before you play; they have

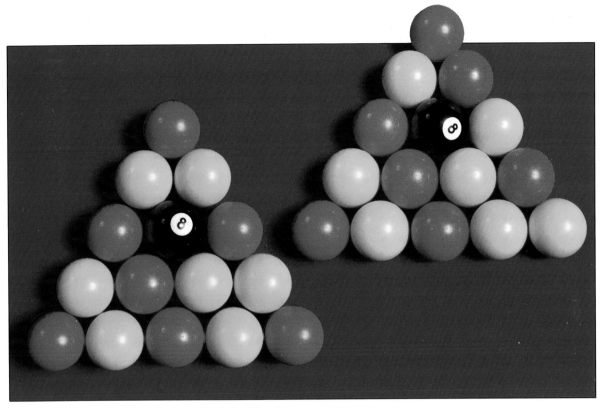

*Standard racking of European pool balls, with colors
alternating around the sides (left); in some clubs and
bars, two balls of the same color are grouped at the top,
two at the bottom, as shown (right).*

the common roots of those in the US, but are amended to suit the table size. The European player is never forgiving of a player who plays *his* game to other's rules.

The way the game is played will be alien to you as well. Your opponent will often pass the opportunity to pocket the object ball if he can place his ball over the pocket. He will play to make you foul-stroke, a game of cat and mouse leaving you frustrated to the point of exasperation. But keep your cool. With a little practice, you can play and beat him at his own game.

The good European pool player will always opt for a finely tapered ½-inch cue tip; the smaller cue ball needs the more precise contact of the smaller tip. Your cue action will need to be lessened; the power you normally use on a medium-pace shot will have the ball leave the table and go into orbit! European pool is played with carefully

taken light- and medium-pace shots dominating play. Power-pace is rarely used except on the break. English and draw also feature widely; even the novice player can have the cue ball behave like a well-trained dog.

The competitiveness of European pool is quite surprising. Prize money is never a great sum and the game evokes only a passing interest in the national TV and press. But this does not deter the player, who plays, not just to win, but to annihilate his opponent, even if the prize is just a pint of favorite beer.

A unique feature of British pool is the work players do at their own time and expense for charity. Over the years, millions of pounds have been donated to a myriad of charities by pool players whose only reward has been a few lines in local newspapers and a deep personal sense of pride in their achievements.

THE
Equipment

Players at one time roughened the cue tip for better contact by rubbing it against a whitewashed ceiling! Things have come a long way since then, with slate bed tables, plastic pool balls and beautifully crafted precision cues.

The table

There are as many different sizes of pool tables as there are manufacturers. This variation is as much to do with the available floor space as it has to do with the floor space allocated! Generally, larger tables are found in clubs, while the smaller ones inhabit spare corners in bars. There isn't an internationally accepted size, although there is a move toward standardizing one for international competitions.

The proportional size of a table is usually half as wide as it is long. The bed is normally slate, although some (thankfully, relatively few) have a composition type. Some tables have siting marks on the rails to help bank shots and positional play, while others are quite plain.

The bed is covered with a tightly stretched cloth, sometimes called baize. There are two basic types of cloth fitted. A natural-fiber cloth with a nap is considered by many to be the best because it can add value to a shot. The alternative is a man-made fiber cloth, which devotees insist is superior because it is napless and does not affect

Check the running of the table and the strength of the banks.

the travel of the cue ball. This increases the value of cue control.

Each table has six pockets and two spots that mark the centre of the foot and head-string lines.

The size of the pockets may vary, depending on the diameter of the balls played. Fortunately, the height of the table is fairly constant.

Shoot Pool is only concerned with the standard US 9 × 4½ft table. The one selected has a blue natural-fiber cloth with a nap, no siting marks on the rails and plays the standard 2¼-inch balls.

Examine each table carefully before you play. Follow a few basic steps and there is less risk you will be caught out by a rogue table. It may take several minutes to inspect a table but it is well worth the trouble.

Start by examining the cloth for nap. The nap runs down the table from the head to the foot. The smoother it is, the faster it will play. Running the flat of your hand over the table by the rails will highlight any damage made by previous careless players. A covering of chalk and dust will often indicate a poorly maintained table, so avoid this table if you can.

Check the nap before you begin: how fast will the table play?

Most tables are quite level, but it is wise to check this as well. Play a lightly paced ball straight down the table center. Any variation of line from the rebound can indicate bias, so play again on another line to be sure.

Check the banks with a squeeze. Soft ones absorb impact and firm ones give a truer return. Note if the banks have an angle, allowing the ball to touch about center.

Finally, check each pocket. The bank should be gently rounded in. If the cloth is threadbare on the pocket fall, it can cause a powerfully pocketed ball to reappear as if by magic.

These simple steps, taken with care, will help your match play and the quality of the game.

Are the pockets in good condition, with the banks gently rounded in?

How do the banks feel to the touch? Are they angled in such a way as to let the ball strike about center?

TABLE GEOMETRY

If you have ever played on a table with markings at regular intervals on the rails, and wondered about their use, the marks are there to help the player accurately calculate the angle a ball will rebound when played as a natural shot. The marks indicate the various (invisible) string lines bisecting the table. The lines running down the table do not have a number but are referred to as the center, left and right lines. The 2-line is known as the string line; the 6-line as the head line. The center line running from the string (2) line and the foot cushion is known as the long line. The foot spot is at the center of the 2-line; the head spot at the center of the 6-line.

The area above the 6-line is referred to as the head area. All games commence with the cue ball being played from any position within the head area. When players "lag" or "string" to determine who plays first, they refer to shots taken from the head (6) line to rebound off the foot bank. The ball returning closest to the head line will determine who plays first.

The banks are just as simple to identify; the head bank, left and right banks, and the foot bank. The complete assembly, wooden frame and bank is known as the rail.

It is usual for only the foot spot to be marked.

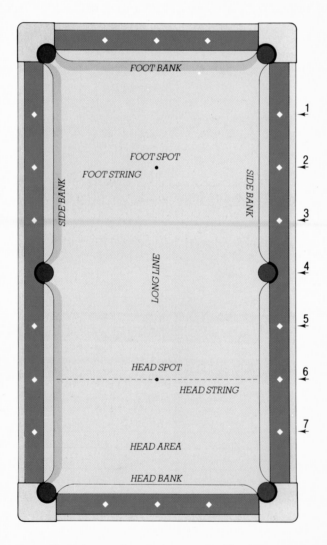

The basic nomenclature for the geography of the table,
which may be useful to refer to when attempting the
exercises which follow later. The standard table is
9 × 4½ft, usually without markings on the banks
indicating the position of the seven invisible string lines.

PURCHASING YOUR OWN POOL TABLE

The dream of having your own table at home is not at all impossible. Cost is not always the criteria; space, or lack of it, is invariably the prime consideration. However, you do not have to live in San Simeon or evict the car from the garage to own a pool table. Manufacturers have come up with some surprising answers to the problem of space limitation . . . and cost.

Never opt for the cheapest table. Some may look the part but few ever play well, far less give lasting pleasure. Always choose a table made by a reputable manufacturer; if you cannot afford a new one, ask if they supply reconditioned tables. Manufacturers offer a wide range of sizes to suit most space restrictions. But for best results never buy a table less than 6 × 3ft; anything smaller will be of little use, a mere toy.

But before you become over-enthused with the idea of owning your own table, it is worthwhile considering three basic, but quite important, questions: Where is the table to set up? What is the access to the area like? Is the floor strong enough?

Most new tables will be assembled in your home by the supplier. Installation is skilled work and is not a job for the family home-handyman. If your finances prohibit professional installation, however, follow the manufacturer's installation sheet exactly. Most good tables arrive in several component pieces to be assembled on site. Moving them into difficult areas is relatively easy, except when it comes to moving the bed. This is usually made from one piece of slate, 1½ inches thick and can weigh up to a quarter of a ton! The edges of the bed will be protected against accidental damage in transit, but when it arrives the protective covers may have to be stripped off to move it in. Slate is not the hardest of materials and a slight knock can cause irreparable damage.

Wherever you decide to position your table, allow a minimum of 4ft all around the table so you can play with ease. Therefore, a 6 × 3ft table will

TABLE CHECKLIST

There follows some basic points to consider when selecting your table:

◊ Avoid tables with composition wood beds; these are prone to warp in damp conditions.

◊ Check that the rails are screwed into position and not glued.

◊ Ascertain whether the cloth covering is natural fiber (with nap) or man-made fiber (napless).

◊ Make certain the table bed size is approximately twice as long as it is wide and the pocket sizes are all the same.

◊ Check that the legs have adjusters to compensate for uneven floors.

◊ If the table you opt for has fold-away legs, make sure that they are properly hinged and are strong enough to prevent the table moving when being played.

◊ Most new tables come with a set of balls; check you have a complete set, the balls are undamaged and, most importantly, they are all the same diameter. If you have to buy a set separately, choose a premium brand. These may cost more but premium balls are weight matched as well.

◊ If purchasing a reconditioned table, a reputable company will provide a guarantee. A good table should have an even bed and firm banks, and should be fitted with a new cloth.

◊ Finally, play a few shots and see how the table plays, then check the guarantee and what it covers exactly.

need an area of 14 × 11ft. Never try to cram the table into a smaller space; the limitations can ruin the pleasure of the game and no-one will be eager to play on your pride and joy!

Choose an area that can easily be reached without going up or down too many stairs. The slate bed will not bend around corners, so it is also advisable to avoid stairs that are too narrow. The fewer problems faced by the installers the easier their task will be, and the risk of damage will be minimized.

Pool tables are never light and you must give careful consideration to this. They are best installed on solid floors. If the table is to go on the first floor or the area has a wooden floor, check with the supplier that the floor will take the weight. Remember, the table will be in one position for a considerable time, and this can seriously affect the stability of the floor structure.

Once you have overcome all of these problems, the real pleasure of your pool room will be apparent. Whatever decor your choose – plush Victoriana, glittering Art Deco or a Scandinavian wood finish – give the room your own personality. Most manufacturers give a choice of color for the cloth covering. If you are a smoker, it is best to have some type of air-conditioning. Keep the room at a fairly constant temperature because extremes in temperature can seriously damage the natural wood of the table.

Always use a light canopy because this low light source prevents your shadow from interfering with play. To complete the set up, make a rack for your cues and, if finances permit, have a selection available for your guests. If you like to serve drinks, make a shelf to stand them on out of harm's way.

CARE OF YOUR TABLE

Treat your table with respect and you will have years of good use from it. Neglect it and very soon it will look shabby and – worse – will become unplayable.

COMMON-SENSE CARE

◊ When you have finished your game, brush the cloth against the nap to remove all the chalk marks, both on the bed and banks. Chalk that is not brushed away will creep into the weave and ruin the nap.

◊ Polish the balls but never leave them racked for the next game. Instead place them in the collecting tray.

◊ Always cover the table when it is not in use. If the cloth looks a little tired, get an expert in to iron and re-stretch it.

◊ From time-to-time, check that the table is level. Use a long spirit level and adjust the legs if necessary. Check the table with a few straight shots until you are happy it plays perfectly.

◊ Never use self-adhesive spots to mark the head and foot spots; a small dot or cross with a felt pen will suffice. Self-adhesive spots may look pretty but they leave a nasty mark on the cloth that is virtually impossible to remove.

◊ There are a number of different chalk cubes available. Choose one that is not too abrasive and matches the color of the cloth. Green and blue chalks are readily available. Other colors are available but may have to be ordered.

THE POOL TABLE MANUFACTURERS

Few sports owe as much to the manufacturers as they do to the participants, but pool is certainly one. Whether they are the Valley Corporation of the US or Hazel Grove Music of Manchester, England, no book about pool is complete without a brief mention of some of the manufacturers that have made pool the game it is today.

A well-maintained table is always a delight to play on, so keep the cloth taut and free from chalk, the wood polished and keep a sheen on the pool balls, which will help to make then run truer. If you are going to invest in your own table, you will also have to buy at least one rest, and preferably both types.

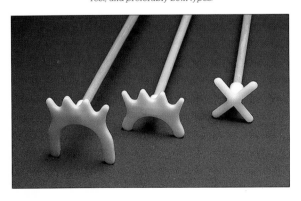

Of course, the demand from players to have a better table has had its effect, otherwise we would still be playing on wood-bed tables with a cloth covering. But the requirements on the manufacturers have always produced equipment far beyond the demand of the players. It is possible to use a composition bed but reputable manufacturers prefer to use fine Italian slate because they believe anything else can affect the way the table plays. Valley could fit cheap cloths but this again will affect the game.

The spread of pool worldwide is particularly due to the farsightedness of the manufacturers and operators. They introduced the game into countries that never had a tradition for table games, and which have, in return, produced world-class players whose efforts add quality and respectability to the game.

Many players argue the manufacturers and operators take too much out of the game. Large, plush offices and showrooms may give the impression of high commercialism, but often the opposite is the truth. Some companies reserve a large annual budget to sponsor pool, bolstering the sport worldwide.

The cue

A cue can be an outward sign of your personality: ornately worked and gem-studded cues, like World Champion Jim Rempe's, or slim and precise like that of World Speed Pool Champion Ross McInnes. Whatever your choice, remember, a cue

If you are going to improve your game, you must have your own cue, and it must be one which feels right to you; the overall weight of the cue, determined by the butt, is the crucial consideration.

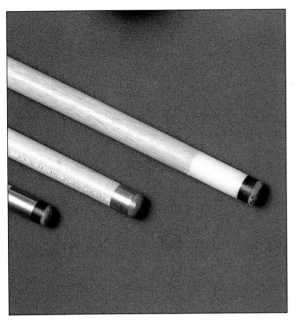

The three types of cue tip: top, slot-on molded; middle, glue-on; bottom, screw-in. No one type is better than any other. The choice is yours.

is the essential tool for good pool play.

Almost all good pool players own their own cues and jealously guard them! Once they have become accustomed to the feel and action of a cue it is rarely changed. Accidental loss or damage can drive the toughest player into a state of near hysteria. So, take a leaf out of their books and purchase your own cue.

Modern cues are made from two woods. The top end is turned from ash or some other straight-grained wood, tapered down to about ⅝ inch, and then spliced to a darker, heavier wood that gives the cue its weight. Traditional, and more expensive cues are made from one complete piece of wood with a weight added in a recess at the butt end. The cheaper club cue is normally made from ramin but this type is liable to warp and fracture as the wood tends to be brittle. The two-part (even four-part) cue is designed to make it easier to carry.

When choosing a cue, check that it is straight above all. Lay it on a flush surface and roll it. The same applies for sectional cues, and also check that the joints screw up flush and firm. The grain should run the full length of the cue. Beware of the cheap cue painted up to resemble an expensive edition. A pretty design is no guarantee of quality.

The choice of the tip end can be quite contentious. Some swear by the screw-in type, others, the complete slot-on molded type and yet more, the glue-on type. The choice is up to you. The tip can be supplied coated in varnish or smooth from molding, and will need roughening up to take the chalk. The tip should be evenly rounded to enable it to make positive contact with the cue ball and may need gently filing down at first. Always check the state of the tip before and during play and chalk it after every shot. A badly shaped or chalked cue tip can ruin the best-planned shot.

Look after your cue. Never lean it against a wall or table between games. Instead, lay it flat. Store it upright in a case, and never leave it in extremes of temperatures or in a damp room. Keep your cue clean by using a damp cloth, and never let it get stained and greasy.

CHALKING YOUR CUE

The contact of the cue on the cue ball is made more positive by chalking the tip. The method of putting chalk on the cue tip is easy. Simply wipe the chalk cube across the tip two or three times, rotating the cue as you do. Look at the tip and if it needs more chalk, add it with the same gentle method. At the same time, inspect the cue tip for any damage or mis-shape. Gently tap the cue to remove any surplus chalk.

The players who use their cues to drill into the chalk cube are doing themselves little favor. While this does add chalk to the tip, it invariably adds too much around the edge of the tip and not always where it is most wanted . . . at the very top. And, no matter how hard they grind the chalk to the tip of their cues, their next shots will often result in a miscue!

The next time you play, look at the chalk cube: if it has a deep crater, ask for a new one.

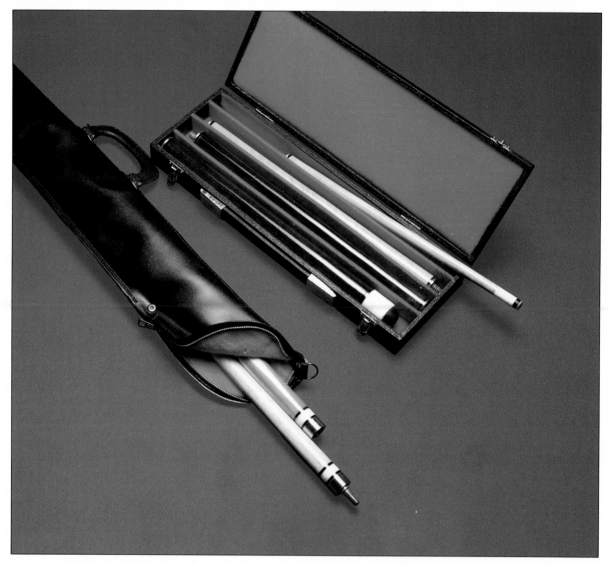

Four-piece and two-piece cues; with sectional cues, it is vital that the joints are flush and firm. The grain should run the full length of the cue.

THE PROFESSIONAL'S CUE

No professional pool player is ever without his own cue. His cue is the tool of his profession and, very often, a great deal of money has been exchanged for the exact specification he believes will give him the edge over his opponents.

The worldwide demand for cues for billiards, snooker and pool, has led some manufacturers to adopt fast production techniques. Such production results in cues with fine action when new but they deteriorate quickly with use. Where wood is turned on a lathe, stress is added and it becomes brittle. The grain may look perfect and straight but the way the wood is worked leaves it weak and very liable to warp.

The alternative is to have your cue made by one of the few 'customizing' professional makers.

There isn't a standard size or weight for a hand-made cue. Selecting a style of cue is the simplest part of the operation. Making the cue to suit the pool player is the art: it must be just the correct weight and length to suit the player and balanced to suit his playing style. Height and weight are the first consideration, then preference of ash or maple. Will the butt be decorated or plain? How many veneers? Will the cue be one piece, two pieces or more? Will it be used abroad or just at home? What ball size will be played? These are just some of the questions that are to be answered before the maker can begin to craft a cue.

The manufacture of hand-made cues is very much in the tradition of the master carpenter. Only the highest quality woods are used – straight grained and fully matured. The cue begins its life as a sawn rectangular "blank." The grain is checked that it runs straight down the length before the maker can begin a lengthy series of hand operations that finally achieves the taper that identifies the hand-made cue from the rest. The blank is planed down in several operations and allowed to settle between each stage. Distortion at any stage will result in the blank being discarded.

After the final planing, each shaft is checked for balance, rigidity and straightness before being cut to the appropriate length.

The butt gives the cue its weight and balance. It is shaped and then joined to the shaft with a hand-made fishtail splice. This system allow the two woods to weld as one and allows the gentlest cue action to feel the contact of cue tip to cue ball. A brass ferrule is fixed to tip of the cue to protect the grain from damage, and then the cue tip is added.

The whole cue is then inspected for quality. Only then will it be converted to a two piece (or more). The screw joints are precision made and when fitted, allow the grain to run naturally the length of the shaft.

Cues selected for the final finishing by craftsmen such as John Parris undergo at least seven sandings with different grades of abrasive, and

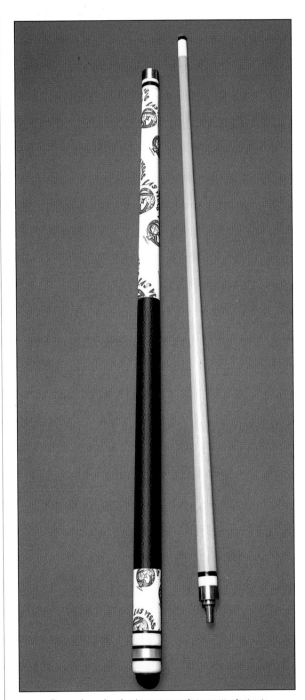

Remember when buying your cue that a pretty design is no guarantee of quality; though this cue is in fact manufactured to a high standard, tapered with painstaking accuracy. When ordering a hand-made cue, expect to answer the following questions: what kind of wood for the shaft – ash or maple? What overall length? What tip size? What kind of butt – diameter and wood? What overall weight? What kind of splicing and what veneers are required?

PERSONALIZED
CUE MANUFACTURE

TOP TO BOTTOM 1 Cue being planed down
for a second pair of ebony splices.
2 The square ash blank, the unspliced shaft and
the finished cue.
3 Fitting the precision brass joint into the butt of
the cue.
4 Cutting a collar on the cue shaft for the brass
ferrule to be fitted.
5 The final hand-sanding prior to polishing.

are then polished with linseed oil to give a silk-like action. The butt is burnished and then waxed.

The final test is the "proof of the pudding" . . . the cue is played on a class table. Only then – when all of the quality checks are made and the maker satisfied – is the new owner allowed to take possession of the cue.

"A cue must be a natural extension of the player. It must feel natural and finely balanced. It should maintain a consistent action throughout its life and never affect the player's game. For a cue to feel 'natural' it must be made from the finest wood and worked on with traditional hand-held tools. Machines may produce thousands of cues in the time it takes me to make just one. But then compare the feel and performance with a hand-made cue. My cues feel and play at least 100 per cent better than any mass-production model."

The cost? Expect to pay around $300 for a hand-made cue.

The pool balls

Fortunately there are not as many sizes of pool balls as there are pool table sizes, but never take it for granted that the size of balls will be the same from city to city. At least ensure the set you are playing is of one size: a quick visual check will confirm this.

A standard pool ball normally has a 2¼-inch diameter, and a set comprises of 16 balls: one white cue ball, eight spot balls (numbered 1–8) and seven stripe balls (numbered 9–15).

The cue ball has been manufactured to be played from the cue action. The object balls play from the impact of one against the other. Never play a shot directly to a stripe or spot ball; not only do they react differently to a cuing action, they can be damaged.

If you play on a coin-operated table, the cue ball may be smaller than the others and you must adjust your game to overcome this oddity. Giving your forward swing more force will add the

Standard 2¼-in diameter American pool balls, made of cast phenolic resin, and (below), their European equivalents. Note that the European cue ball is smaller than the object balls, because it is used on a coin-operated table. Obviously, an adjustment of power and pace is required when playing with a smaller cue ball.

necessary pace to the cue ball to move the larger object ball.

Before you lag, inspect the balls for any damage. If a ball is cracked or pitted, change it. If the balls look dull, give them a polish with a damp cloth. Pool is best played when the balls sport a fine sheen because this reduces their friction on the cloth and makes them play truer.

THE Skills

Pool is a fast, skillful and entertaining game; but as with all games, the higher your standard, the more satisfying it is to play. It is surprising therefore, just how many people do not try to improve their skills, but are content to stick with the same old shots, the same old mistakes. Don't be one of the crowd! Take charge of your game, and with a few simple exercises, exploit the whole gamut of techniques and strategies which pool has to offer.

Introduction

If you have ever watched a professional game of pool, you will have seen players demonstrating their various skills in cue- and cue-ball control, together with planned gamesmanship and sometimes pure theater. This is the essence of pool and highlights the aggressive competitiveness the game can bring out.

Pool play was highly publicized in films such as *The Hustler* and *The Color of Money*, but they did little justice to ordinary people for whom pool is a way of life. Admittedly there is money in the game – side bets on local club games and megabucks being won in top world championship competitions – but never be misled. These games are just side shows compared with those being played every day by thousands of people from all walks of life. They shoot pool for the love of the game, and it is part-and-parcel of their social life. Sons play fathers, and daughters as well are taking to the game . . . resulting in the emergence of national women's pool teams, often eclipsing the standards of their male counterparts.

If you see yourself as a potential Fast Eddie, be prepared to have someone break your fingers. If your ideal is to become the state champion or even a future world champion, go to a top club and watch the professionals. Their games are miles above those played by local club players, full of obvious planning, skillful cue work and incredible match play. They seem to be able to make a clearance from nothing, to pot from impossible angles. Their play is natural and polished.

The practice before any serious match play is taken very seriously. Daily six-hour practice sessions to keep cuing action and match-play skills constantly near perfection are not unusual. Make this dedication your standard and take a leaf out of their book. Practice makes perfect.

Only with constant and planned practice will you ever be able to achieve any good standard of pool play. If you already play and aspire to greater

Jim Rempe, winner of world and grand championship titles in the US, England, Japan, Sweden, Australia and New Zealand.

heights, *Shoot Pool* is the book for you. The exercises are not drawn from just one person's play but are a compilation of various attitudes and styles drawn from many years playing and observing.

Pool is a fast-developing game and every day yet another version hits the tables. Speed pool is now an international game. Fifteen-ball pool and the latest gem, 9-ball pool, are growing in popularity wherever pool players congregate. The Japanese are taking to the game like ducks to water. The Europeans have taken pool and made it their own with specially designed tables, thinly tapered cues with ⅝-inch tips and a host of complicated match play rules.

As the game progresses, the manufacture and quality of the equipment increases. Manufacturers are constantly finding new methods to improve the quality and style of pool equipment, and it is largely due to them that the game is so finely structured. Without the rules to set the structures of the game, pool would not exist in the way it does today.

THE SHOTS AND THEIR DESCRIPTIONS

To eliminate any confusion from the descriptions of the various shots and cue actions described here, the terminology used is from when pool was in its infancy. Terms such as "English" and "draw" were commonplace when pool was being played as early as 1910. Banks were banks before they became cushions. If you shoot pool, these terms may be foreign to begin with, probably at complete variance to those you are used to. For the novice, the terms will appear quite natural and need no further explanation.

If you use the practice exercises as they have been designed, your play and knowledge of pool will expand.

Cue control

All match play skills originate from the way the cue is controlled. It is vital to understand that three elements – stance, grip and cue action – are combined together on one cohesive movement to give this control.

This chapter provides the model from which to build and adopt your own style. Novices should read the directions with an open mind. Someone who already shoots pool, should open their mind first, then read the directions. The position for a steady stance, how to keep a firm grip, and the action for a fluent swing to cue action are all difficult to adopt at first, but persevere. Soon the benefits to your game will be well worth the effort.

Stance

All good players know they must stand firm and balanced. The only movement to make is the cue action, a smooth swing coming from the shoulder and elbow joints.

If you *think* your stance is firm enough, ask a friend to give you a gentle push on the shoulders.

A wobble, even very slight, is a clear indication your stance is wrong. Correct this fault before any other.

The following exercise shows how to adopt a firm stance at the table (presuming you are right handed):

Stand to the table at 90 degrees from the center line and place your left hand on the table about half-way between the head string and the head bank. Hold the cue in your right hand and rest it on your hand on the table. Bend at the waist and move back, keeping the cue parallel to the table. As you move back, your weight will be thrown forward and taken by your hand on the table. Hold your right arm tight to your body and bend it only at the elbow, swinging it back as you bend your body. Move back until you feel your lower right arm make a right angle with the cue. Move your feet about 8 inches apart. Move your left leg forward slightly and bend it at the knee. Keep your right leg straight and twist your foot out of line. At this point your head will be forward, so keep your head up and look directly down the table; your chin should not be more than 12 inches

Your stance will depend partly on your height; but your chin should never be more than twelve inches above the cue. Take your right arm back until it makes a right-angle with cue. This is the correct position for lining up the shot, and the basis of all good pool play.

It is impossible to give exact instructions as to stance which will be right for everyone; but here, it might be suggested that the player is standing too far from the table and is stretching for the shot, with too great a distance between the bridge and the cue tip.

above the cue. The photograph shows just how easy this contortion is with practice.

It is important, however, not to stand too erect with your stance, and to aim your cue accurately. Unless you are a trick shooter, aiming cue action from hip level can produce only trick shots. A correct stance will give direction to the cue action. Keep your right arm tucked tight to your body and don't let it wander out like a penguin's flipper. The direction the cue swings will control the direction of the cue ball. A smooth, straight swing is what is needed.

It's impossible to give directions for every player of every size. Follow the way the stance is best achieved, then adjust the final position to suit yourself, remembering the basic principles. If you are left-handed, read left for right in the above directions.

When you are comfortable with your new stance ask your friend to give you yet another gentle push on the shoulders. If you move again, your stance is still wrong, so begin over. Always remember never to have your feet too far apart and never over-reach to make a shot when taking your stance. Keep your cue action smooth and accurate.

The cue grip

The cue is a light, precision piece of worked wood, and there is no need to hold like a riot stick. Hold the cue about two inches from the butt end with a firm grip then relax the hold but keep your fingers curled. Grip the cue in the arc of your thumb and first finger and let the other fingers add enough pressure to hold the cue to your palm.

The reason for a light but firm grip is very simple. A light grip lets you "feel" the contact of the cue and cue ball more accurately. It also allows your wrist enough movement to follow the swing of the arm. An overtight grip stiffens your wrist, impedes the swing and dulls the "feel."

The bridge arm

Place your hand on the table, stretch it out and twist it slightly at the elbow, then relax. This transfers your weight, thrown forward by your stance, to your bridge hand. How far you bend your arm depends on the distance you are cuing from and how tall you are.

The bridge hand

This first bridge is referred to as the normal bridge and has been designed to aim your cue easily to play a natural shot. Lay your hand palm flat on the table, then spread your fingers apart. Raise your hand with your fingers still on the cloth and evenly spaced apart. Press down gently on your hand and feel your fingertip-grip on the cloth tighten. Raise your thumb and press it forward into the side of your first finger; your hand will now be bent and slightly flexed. Adopt your stance, grip your cue and lay it in the "V" of your thumb and first finger and adjust the height of your bridge to allow you to play the cue ball dead-center while keeping your cue parallel to the table . . . you are almost ready to take a shot.

If you need to select a low target on the cue ball, lay your hand flat on the cloth, spread your fingers and roll your hand until it rests on the heel. Raise your thumb, keep it close to your first finger to make the cuing "V." You have made a low bridge.

The third hand bridge, the high "V" is described later in the book. It has only a few specific uses and will be covered in the cue ball-control section.

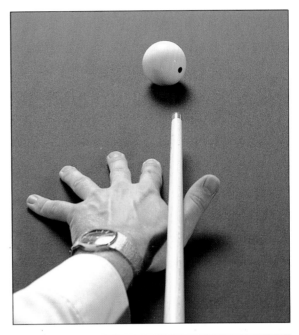

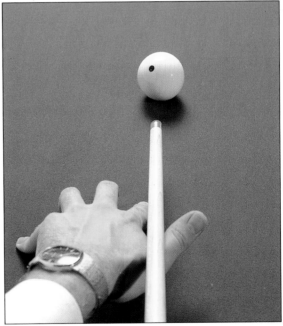

TOP To select a low target on the cue ball, the heel of the hand must rest on the table and the fingers should be well spaced, to form the low bridge.

ABOVE AND LEFT The normal bridge, with the hand raised and the fingers evenly spaced pressing down on the cloth.

The cue action

This is a simple three-part motion. It has been developed to give you time to aim, to check the aim and to play a well-controlled shot.

To appreciate the movements, take them one at a time. When you are familiar with all of them, put them together and you will have a precise cue action.

The first part is to *aim the cue* in the direction of the shot, through your arm, over the "V" of the bridge and through the cue ball to the object ball. Next, *swing your cue back* until your grip is almost under your shoulder. Now pause and check the direction of the cue. Finally, when you are sure that your aim is correct, swing the cue forward.

The forward swing will bring the cue-tip into contact with the cue ball, and it is vital the cue movement follows the line of shot exactly and is kept parallel to the table. Continue the forward swing through, past the point of impact (rather like a stroke in golf) and stop it a few inches beyond where the cue ball would have been.

The whole forward swing of the cue action must be as precise and well oiled as a piston stroke. If you let your elbow swing out your shot will be inaccurate. Don't bring your body up as you swing through, because this can add extra, unwanted power to the shot. When you have completed the shot, don't lay there admiring your handiwork, straighten up before the rebounding ball strikes your clothing or cue.

The other cue action is the stab shot and this is described in the cue ball-control section. Do not attempt this shot until your cue action is under control. The stab shot is used under the most dire conditions.

AIM, BACKWARD AND FORWARD SW...

1, 2, 3 Line up the shot, with the cuing arm at ninety degrees to the cue, sighting down the cue, through the cue ball to the object ball.

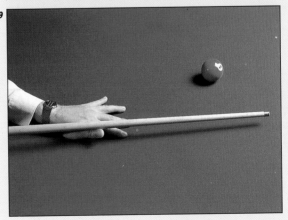

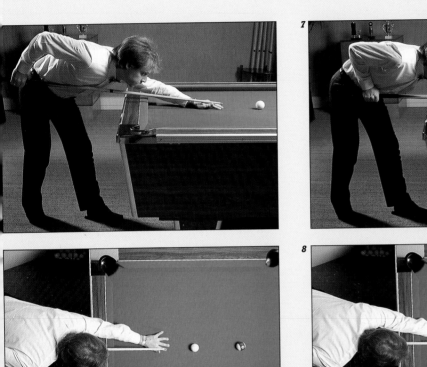

4, 5, 6 Swing back the cue and pause to adjust direction, ensuring that the cue tip will make contact exactly in the center of the cue ball, for a natural shot.

7, 8, 9 Keep your forward swing evenly paced, and follow through past the point of impact so that the cue tip comes to rest a few inches beyond where the cue ball would have been.

Stance, grip and cue action as one

Put all three components together. Make sure the complete stance is comfortable . . . you are ready, at last, to play a shot.

ABOVE In many ways, the moment just before the forward swing begins is the most important in the whole game, when final adjustments are made. If you hesitate too long, you may lose balance and concentration; if you rush the shot, you will lose control. If you are not absolutely sure what you are trying to do at that moment, then step back and take your stance again. Like most games, pool is won and lost in the head.

HEAD STILL, HAND FIRM, SWING EVEN

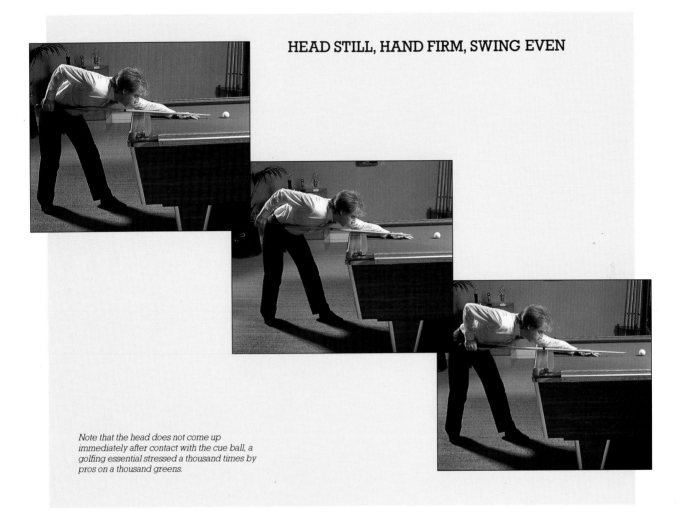

Note that the head does not come up immediately after contact with the cue ball, a golfing essential stressed a thousand times by pros on a thousand greens.

Cue ball control

The primary function of your stance is to accurately control the direction the cue ball travels when you play it. Only when you can exercise this control will your game improve and develop.

Place the cue ball on the head spot, make a normal bridge and play the ball straight down the table, through the foot spot to the foot bank and return to the head of the table via the same route. If you can successfully play this simple exercise six or seven times in succession, your knowledge of cue ball control can begin to improve.

41

Controlling the momentum of the cue ball

In many circles the forward momentum of the cue ball after making a shot, and before it hits an object ball or bank, is called pace.

The accuracy of your shot has two components, direction and pace. Direction you have practiced; pace is the amount of power you add through your cue action to make the cue ball travel a given distance. Your appreciation of pace is as vital as the straightness of your shot, and learning it is relatively easy.

Ask permission to make a few light chalk marks on the cloth; one center table opposite the center pockets, another on the foot bank in line with the head and foot spots and another half way between the mark opposite the pockets and the head spot. Four marks in all, and make sure that you mark them *lightly*.

Pace can be governed in five distinct ways: place the cue ball on the head spot and play straight down the table:

1. Light-pace Play the ball to move no further than the mark between the center pockets.

2. Medium-pace Play the ball to stop at the foot spot.

3. Moderate-pace Play the ball to the mark on the foot bank, rebound and stop no further than the foot spot.

4. Strong-pace Play the ball down the table to hit the mark on the foot bank and return no further than the mark between the center pockets.

5. Power-pace Play the ball to rebound off the mark on the foot bank to the head bank and return down the table to stop near the center pockets, and then the foot bank. Power-pace is a crude cue action, and if used out of control will ruin your game.

This exercise will help you to appreciate pace. Play only at first to achieve light-pace, then move through to strong-pace. When you can confidently position the cue ball from each exercise, extend the practice session to achieve different pace shots in various orders: light, power, medium, power and so on.

Pace is not just the effort required to play a natural shot. It is also the effort needed to play the cue ball to an object ball, and move the object ball to a given distance after impact. A shot with light-pace will move the object ball to just short of the position the cue ball would have stopped when played with a straight shot. Begin your practice with this pace and vary the distance apart you place the cue and object balls. With controlled pace, the cue ball should slow and virtually stop on impact with the object ball when it is placed on the mark that shows the maximum the cue ball should travel with a given pace.

TOP AND ABOVE Keep the table clear to give you clean lines for judging pace in these early simple exercises. Pace depends upon length and speed of swing, and cleanness of contact with the cue ball.

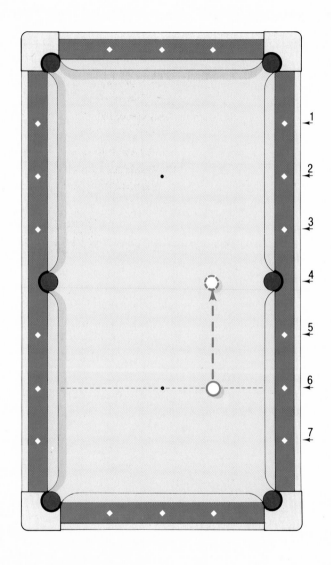

Without using an object ball to begin with, play the cue ball from the head string to come to rest between the center pockets. It may look just a little too easy for an expert like you, but it is extremely interesting just how many people who have been playing pool for years can't do it!

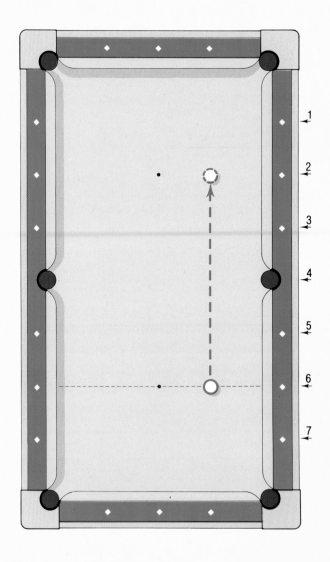

1
2
3
4
5
6
7

Play the ball from the head string to come to rest at the
foot spot. Obviously, part of the discipline of these
exercises lies in striking the cue ball dead-center, and
ensuring that it travels in a perfectly straight line
parallel to the banks.

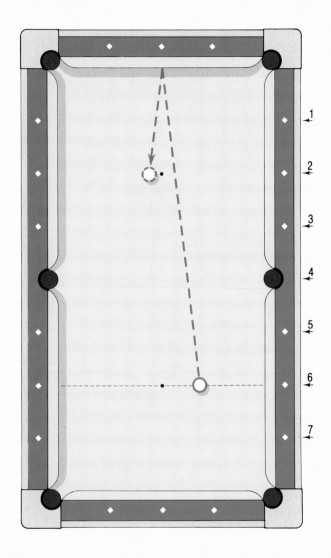

*From the head string to the foot bank and back to the
foot spot; this time, angle the ball slightly to ensure that
you are imparting absolutely no spin to the cue ball –
and aim to leave the cue ball on the foot spot, not just
anywhere along the foot string.*

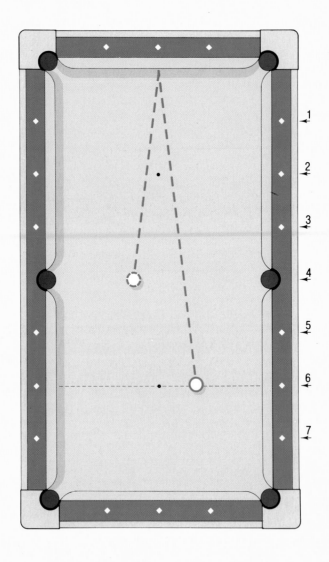

1

2

3

4

5

6

7

*Far more difficult: aim for the exact center of the foot
bank, and bring the cue ball to rest no further than the
center string. Practice by approaching the center
string – that is, by employing too little pace rather than
too much.*

● EXERCISE 5 ●
POWER PACE

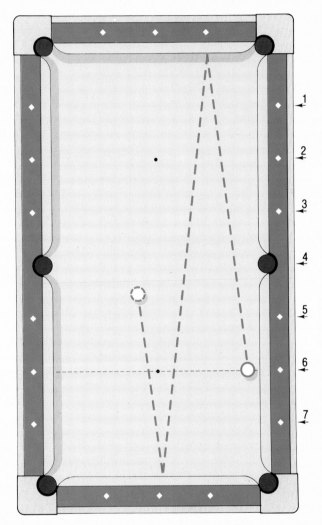

Probably about as much power as you will ever have to impart to the cue ball in a game situation – except perhaps in the break. Steve Mizerak uses a heavier cue solely for the break . From the head string to the foot bank, then back off the head bank to rest between the center pockets, and then on to the foot string – again, without imparting any spin, draw, or English to the cue ball (these terms are explained later, but basically they are what happens when you don't target the ball in the center, in this case with almost certainly disastrous results). The firmness of the banks can obviously make a tremendous difference to the "accuracy" of this kind of shot. If possible, avoid it in a game situation.

Now use an object ball to measure your pace: when employing medium pace as in this example, the cue ball should stop on impact on the foot spot.

Extend the practice by using medium-pace and vary it by alternating light- and medium-pace.

Using moderate- and strong-pace will require you to play down the table at a slight angle to avoid the cue and object ball colliding. When the object ball strikes the bank it will lose some of the pace and the return will fall short of the mark. Depending on the condition of the foot bank, this could be as much as 25 per cent. Using this slightly angled shot may complicate the exercise but it is

When attempting a power shot, always target the cue ball dead center; here the bridge hand may be too low, and the ball will be out of control and may well leave the table.

essential to use it to understand these more forceful shots. Make sure the angle you cue at is small enough to allow the object ball a clear passage up the table without striking any side banks.

Now, practice the power-pace shot. This is essentially a crude shot, and, crude through it is, it must be played in full control. Play to have the cue ball hit both the foot and head cushions and stop near the foot spot. The closer it gets, the more control there is, but achieving it after collision with two banks is very difficult.

Always target the cue ball dead center. Many players will use the power-pace without any real idea of control, sometimes sending the cue ball off the table and into orbit after impact with the object ball.

PACE AND TABLE DIMENSIONS

Part of the enjoyment of shooting pool comes from being able to pick up a cue and play in any of the thousands of venues across the world. The only thing that can mar your enjoyment will be the numerous sizes of tables that you will be confronted with.

It is no simple matter to play on a table smaller (or larger) than the size you are used to. Some players, when faced with a different size table, cannot adjust their forward swing, and this often results in a game far below their normal expectations. If you do not want to fall into this trap, practice on varying size tables; never concentrate on just the table size at the local club or even the one you have at home.

Compensating for different size tables is easy in theory but quite difficult in execution. Obviously, on a table smaller than your usual one, less force is needed in your forward swing to achieve the various pace shots; more force for a larger table.

Once you have conquered the pace shots on your normal table, find another size table to extend your practice. If you are able to adjust quickly to a different size table you can at least compete on an equal level with the local players. You will certainly have a head start on an unwary opponent.

Natural shots

One of the immediate aims in shooting pool is to pocket the object ball. The easiest way to determine how accurate your stance, cue action and aim are is to align the cue and object balls to a pocket and play a shot to pocket. If you fail in this simple test, go back to chapter One!

First play across the table to the center pockets. Don't worry at this stage if the cue ball follows the object ball into the pocket, the next chapter explains how cue ball control will stop this happening.

Play diagonally across the table, down the table from left to right. If your medium-pace is working well, the cue ball will not disappear from sight. Increase the difficulty by using a smaller angle of play each time until you are virtually playing parallel to the side banks.

Shooting to pocket is an important part of pool. Don't move on further until you can achieve a success rate of at least nine out of 10 shots. Even then you will only be almost efficient at pocketing!

The shot played at an angle

Now that the natural shot is within your grasp, learn to cue at an angle to the object ball so it moves in a given angle away from the impact point.

Determining the angle of deflection is not a skill players are born with, nor is it a matter of simple mathematics. The angle of deflection the object ball travels after impact is governed by the angle of the line of play and the pace. Add to that the condition of the nap and the state of the balls, and mathematical calculations become too complicated to solve easily!

Predict where to strike the object ball to move it to the left or right off the line of play after impact from the cue ball, and commit the results to memory. Rarely are two angle shots the same.

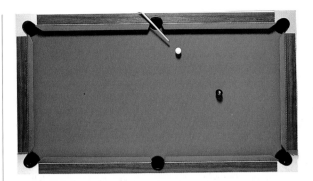

TOP A natural shot played to the corner pocket.
MIDDLE Slightly angled shot, calling for three-quarter face contact.
BOTTOM Fine cut to the center pocket; actually probably an easier shot than the one above it, despite the more extreme angle, because of the proximity of the object ball to the pocket.

The distance the balls are apart will vary as much as the precise angle, leaving you with a vast array of possibilities to carry around in your head. As each new situation arises, add it to your store of angles; there is no textbook way of storing all this information. But take heart – pool was devised for pool players.

Angle shots sometimes look impossible, but some of the difficulty is removed by the size of the

Both of these shots will need about the same pace: because the angle is more acute on the shot above, the area of impact is less, and so the pace needed is more than for a straighter shot. But the distance to the pocket is also less.

pockets, giving a reasonable chance of pocketing even if the shot is slightly off line.

There are five cardinal impact points on the object ball, and these begin to be counted off as the line of play passes from straight to left or right of the object ball. These contact points refer to the point on the face of the object ball the cue ball must strike in order to move the object ball in a given direction, as follows:

1. Full-face contact is the result of an accurate natural shot (which you control precisely), and is made when the cue ball strikes the object ball exactly in the center down a straight line of play.

4. Three-quarter face (¾-face) contact will move the object ball 5–30 degrees to left or right.

3. Half-face (½-face) contact will move the object ball 30–60 degrees to the right or left.

2. Quarter-face (¼-face) contact will move the object ball 60–80 degrees to the right or left.

This session highlights any flaws you have in making natural shots. Keep the illustration handy as you begin to practice. Place the balls on the

table as illustrated and begin to make the angle shots in rotation. When you feel confident enough, move the balls further apart and begin the sequence again. Place a ball over the center pocket and pocket it from various angles.

In a match situation, the direct line to the object ball is often covered by your opponent's ball. The part of the object ball you can see will be less than full face and the impact will give the same result as the angle shot, and your knowledge of the angle from impact the object ball will take will help give a value to the shot.

5. The fine cut is the last angle shot to consider, and is the most extreme. With skill, a player can move the object ball almost at right angles.

The cue ball is targeted to the extreme edge of the object ball to achieve this most delicate shot.

The basic problem with the fine cut is that you will have to use a little more power in your forward swing to give the cue ball more pace, because the angle of impact is so small. A normal-pace ball might not move the object ball enough to gain from the shot.

To appreciate the shot, place an object ball about 3 inches out from the center of the pocket. Place the cue ball on the head string, 4 inches away from the bank, and play it natural with medium-pace.

As you repeat the exercise, move the object ball further out from the pocket and the cue ball out from the bank. You will soon be aware that the further you want to move the object ball from impact, the more power you must give to your forward swing.

The fine-cut shot is designed to move the object ball in a narrow arc of between 80–90 degrees and about 7 inches away from the point of impact. The closer the point of impact is to the edge of the object ball, the finer the cut will be. But beware: the fine-cut will need extra pace to play because the slight impact from ball to ball is lessened by the fineness of the cut. You can easily ruin the game by a sudden attack of power-pace if you try to move the object ball any further than 7 inches.

● *EXERCISE 6* ●
FULL-FACE CONTACT

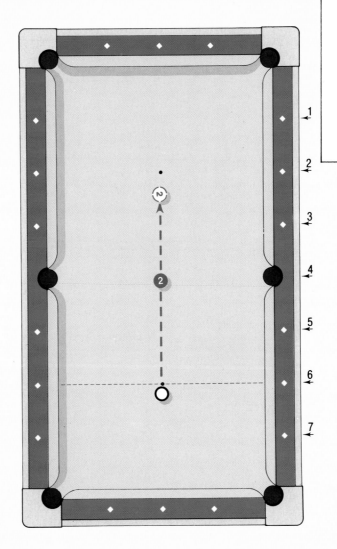

You must be able to make contact with the object ball in
a perfectly straight line before you can hope to master
the angled shot. Concentrate on the line of impact
through the center of cue ball and object ball, and aim
at first to move the object ball no more than a quarter of
a table-length: feel the amount of pace required and
remember it.

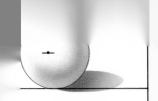

● EXERCISE 7 ●
THREE-QUARTER FACE
CONTACT

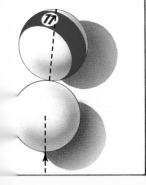

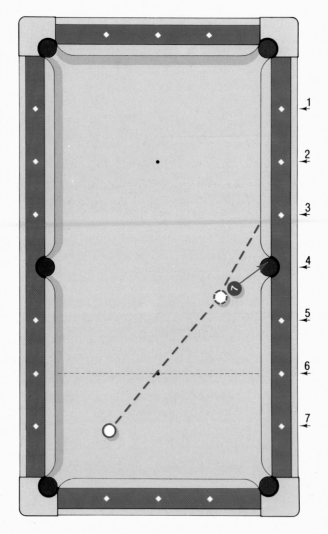

1 ◄
2 ◄
3 ◄
4 ◄
5 ◄
6 ◄
7 ◄

*Place the object ball no more than six inches from the
center pocket, and concentrate upon the line of impact
required once more. Be aware of where the cue ball
comes to rest after impact.*

● *EXERCISE 8* ●
HALF-FACE CONTACT

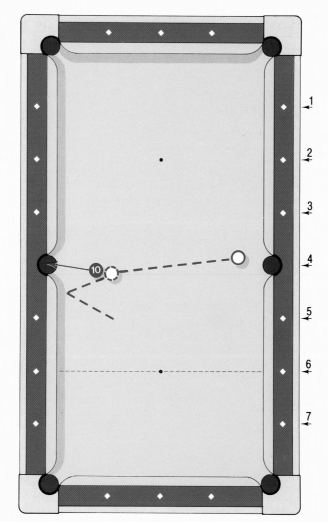

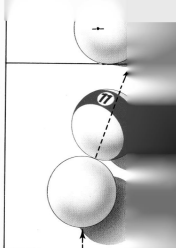

A 30- to 60-degree angle is the result of half-face contact. Slightly more pace is required because of the smaller area of impact, and the cue ball will certainly come back off the bank in the situation illustrated: just how much it comes back may make the difference between an easy next shot and defeat, in a game situation.

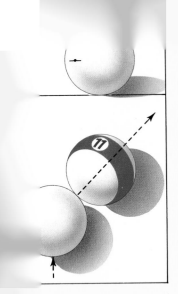

● EXERCISE 9 ●
QUARTER-FACE
CONTACT

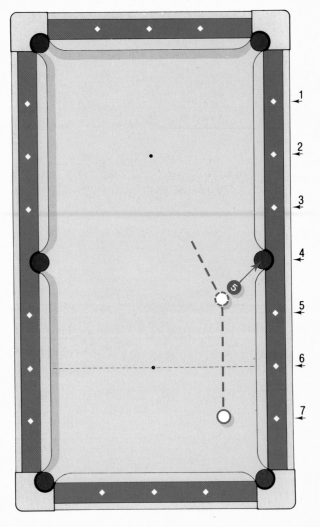

*For a 60- to 80-degree angle; it is now that a knowledge
of Newton's second law – or at least a clear mental
picture of the lines of force acting upon the object ball
as shown in the diagram above left – comes into play. If
the object ball is much more than a foot from the
pocket, control of the cue ball after the shot becomes
very difficult.*

● EXERCISE 10 ●
THE FINE CUT

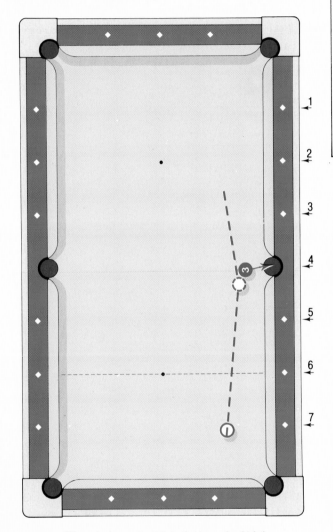

*When playing a natural shot – that is, one in which the
cue ball is struck exactly in the center – it is actually
physically impossible to move the object ball at a full 90
degrees from the point of contact with the cue ball, but
you can get very close. The greatest danger is in
forcing the shot to compensate for the lack of contact
area, thereby risking possibly unnecessary and
potentially disastrous power play, sending the cue ball
hurtling off who knows where. Clearly, the closer the
object ball to the pocket, the easier it is to control the
cue ball.*

Playing off the banks

So far your shots have been played directly from cue to object ball. Now you must learn to bend the line of play by using the banks. The cue ball loses some of its pace when rebounding off the bank, so bear this in mind when playing to them. Using the banks to make contact with your object ball is a primary defensive shot. As with the deep swerve and the masse (later described in depth), this shot is played when the direct line to your object ball is blocked by an opposing ball. Unlike the other two shots, playing off the bank is a little more predictable – unless you use spin or back-spin.

PREDICTING THE ANGLE OF REBOUND

The illustration shows how to use the diamond markers on the bank rails to help predict the angle a ball will take after hitting a bank. The diagram is based on a 9 × 4½ft table. The diamond system is based on the predicted angle of rebound from a natural shot.

You can appreciate the usefulness of this diagram if you can play a three-bank shot. Play the shot from over the left-hand top pocket to the 6-string. Play with a strong-pace, natural shot; you should hit three banks before the ball comes to rest, about level with the 3-string line.

If you play a natural shot to a bank, it will rebound off at the same but opposite angle of impact. If the banks are firm, very little of the pace will be lost by the impact and the ball will be returned at about the same pace. The marks on the rails have a secondary, and perhaps, more important function than just indicating the various string lines; they also help the player judge the angle of rebound of a ball played to the bank.

Many players rely on their experience and use the marks just for reference. To the novice or aspiring player they are vital. And if the table doesn't have any markings, ask permission to make light chalks marks in their place.

You may see players marking a target spot on the bank with the cue tip. This is a particularly stupid habit because it can damage the cloth covering, and in some competitions, such markings are illegal. When you mark the banks, do it lightly and brush them off when you have finished.

If you look at the diagram (right) you will see that the diamond system is easy to follow. It relies upon the ball being played naturally ; English and draw will profoundly affect the angle of rebound. Practice using the basic diagram with medium- and moderate-paced shots. The greater number of banks the ball has to rebound off will reduce the pace with each consecutive impact. Play first to impact one cushion. Target the spot carefully and play until you can hit it expertly. When you have succeeded, increase to using two, three and eventually four banks.

Only after you have learned the pace to make these banked shots can you attempt to pocket from them. Place an object ball over the center-right pocket and play from the 2-string line. The pace you use for the shot should keep the cue ball from dropping into the pocket as well. Only play more adventurous shots when you can fully control the cue ball and keep it out of the pocket.

When you are really competent, play the five bank shot ... some call it a "five bank cocked hat." When you can pocket from it with some degree of success, add it to your repertoire of shots to impress.

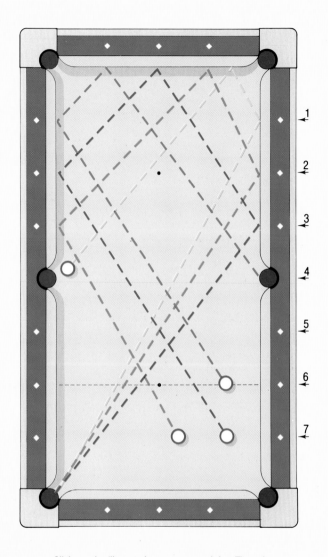

All the angles illustrated assume a natural shot. Through practicing them many times, you will soon find that you have drawn for yourself a kind of mental map of the table which you can instinctively refer to in game situations. The joy of pool of course, is that when all the object balls are in play, the number of angles becomes more or less infinite, so that no two shots following the break are ever exactly the same.

● EXERCISE 11 ●
POWER PLAY OFF
THREE BANKS

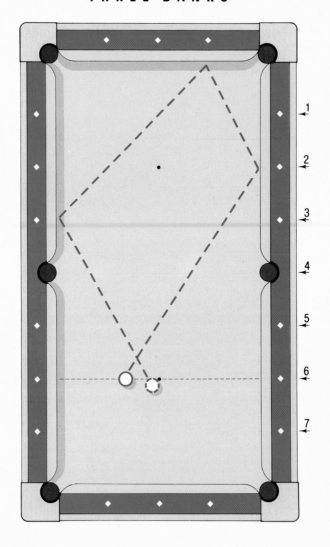

*Once you have practiced the earlier exercises enough,
and have studied the diamond system on the preceding
page, power pace shots off three banks like this can be
approached with real intent to pot a ball or play to
safety.*

● EXERCISE 12 ●
THE SIMPLE
BANKED SHOT

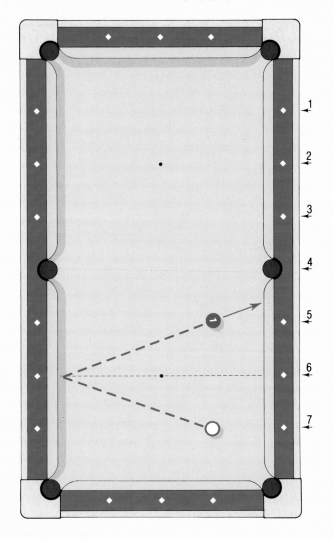

The most commonly used banked shot: short, and off
one bank. You will probably have to attempt it many
times over a series of games, so practice it now. To
begin with, be content simply to make contact with the
object ball, but as your confidence increases, go for
your shots: pot the ball, or aim to play away to safety.

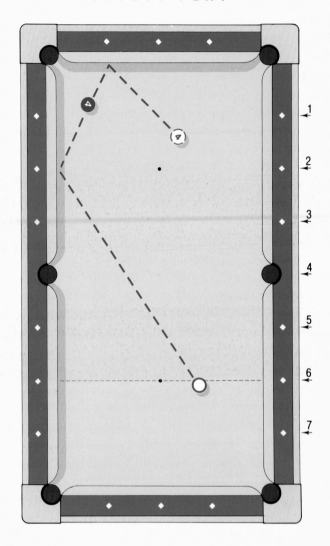

Send the cue ball from the head string off the center of the side bank to take the object ball off the foot bank so that it comes to rest around the foot spot. The discipline here is in attempting full-face contact between cue ball and object ball, so that the cue ball follows the object ball and comes to rest against the foot bank; thus leaving your opponent with a difficult bridge.

● EXERCISE 14 ●
THE DOUBLE
BANKED SHOT

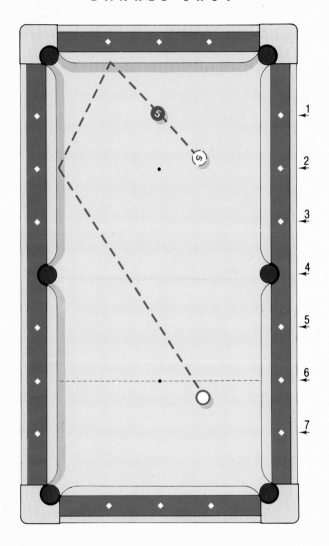

*From the head string off the center of the side bank and
foot bank to make full-face contact with the object ball.
The difference in the resilience of the banks of different
tables can be very marked. A few double-banked
practice shots before a game will quickly give you a
feel for their condition.*

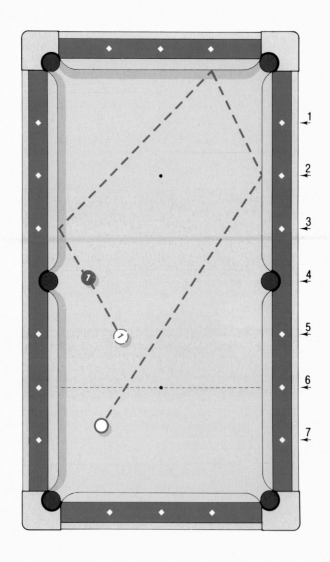

*Unusual in a game situation, but great practice – and
you will occasionally be faced with it for real. Once
again, the best basis for the exercise is to aim for full-
face contact with the object ball. Remember the
diamond system, and use markers on the banks to help
map out the angles.*

● EXERCISE 16 ●
FOUR BANK SHOT

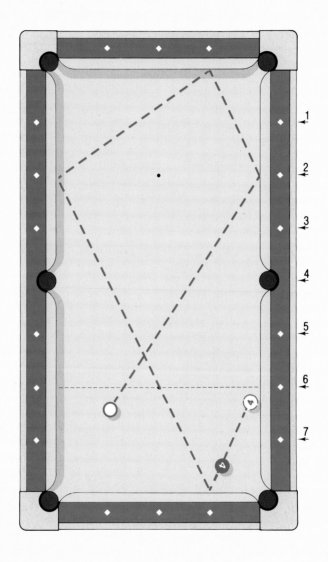

*How many times can you succeed in executing this shot
in a row? Twice? Three times? Keep practicing! Try for
a "high run" of five or six. If you succeed, be assured
that your game is really hotting up.*

*Nick Varner (**BELOW**) and Willie Hoppe (seen here at the billiard table) using the index finger for extra control of the cue; a few players prefer this type of bridge.*

Awkward cue action and bridging

These next sections deal with the occasions when your normal, well-oiled cue action, and even your bridge, will not be sufficient for the task. The stab action will stop short your cue action and the high "V" will torture your fingers and wrist. These are all part of cue control and you will have to use them in certain situations.

THE STAB CUE ACTION

There are occasions when you will have to stop short the forward swing of your cue action, particularly when the follow through might take in the cloth and table bed as well.

When you play a stab shot, the forward swing must stop the moment your cue strikes the cue ball. You may have to tighten your cue grip to add extra control, and this will have the effect of adding extra power to the swing. Always remember this when you play the stab shot.

AWKWARD BRIDGE POSITIONS

During any game there will be a time when your normal bridge will not be sufficient to play the shot. To be in a position where you have to make these awkward bridges is all part of shooting pool, and it is a measure of your pool skill how you resolve it. According to the situation, you may have to use the awkward high "V," cue off the bank rails, or use the mechanical "V." Each will have some effect on the quality of the shot and, given the difficulty of the position, alter the outcome of the game. It is important to become familiar with these awkward bridges to increase the quality of the difficult shots that require them.

Stab cue action and high "V"; note how the wrist is flexed and how the cue tip cannot, even with such a high bridge, make contact through the center of the cue ball.

CUE DOWN THE BANK

When the cue ball is close to the bank, place your bridge hand on the bank rail, form a low bridge, use your first finger to steady the position by curling it over the bank and play the shot. You will tend to aim slightly higher than normal and you can have a tendency to hit the cue ball high above center and encourage the cue ball to overrun the object ball. When the cue ball is further down the table, to avoid using the mechanical "V," it is often best to lay slightly on the bank rail with one leg. This is legal but make sure your other foot keeps contact with the floor. In this position you will have to extend your bridge arm almost straight and use a very low bridge.

Low bridge with cue ball tucked up against the bank.

CUE BALL FROZEN ON THE BANK

If you cue directly across the table, you will have only a tiny part of the top of the cue ball to target. Regardless of how you play, you will add top-English to the ball with the resultant over-run of the object-ball position. Use a low bridge, play well back from the table and use only light pace.

The situation is lessened if you play down the table when the cue ball is frozen . . . but only by a fraction. You will have to cue at an angle to the table and use a high "V" bridge combined with a stab shot. For this shot, stand close to the table and ignore your normal stance. Form the high "V" and play with light-pace; any harder and you will give the ball a deep swerve action.

Stab cue action and high "V" with the cue ball against the bank can easily impart deep swerve.

CUE ACROSS THE BANK RAIL

When the cue ball lays three inches or more from the bank rail you can use the firmest and most popular bridge. Make your normal bridge on the bank rail but this time move the cue between the first and second fingers. Keep those fingers close together but not so close to impede the smoothness of the swing. Most shots can be played from this position. Some players don't like it because they prefer not to lose the feel of the cue between thumb and first finger.

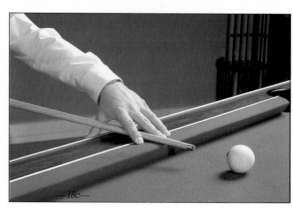

Cuing across the bank rail, when the cue ball is at least three inches from the bank.

THE HIGH "V"

This bridge is the one most players avoid at all costs. The stance places them out of balance, the grip is different and the resulting shot rarely gains more than just striking the object ball. The cue is held at about 45 degrees to the table: You must make a stab shot and target above the center line of the cue ball. Make the bridge with your hand, this time extending the fingers straight and close together. To gain height for this shot, raise your stance by bending your right foot and take partially the weight on the ball of your foot. Your full weight will be far forward and taken on the extended fingers of your bridge hand. Play the stab shot with medium-pace unless you are making a deep-screw shot.

The high "V"; body weight is inevitably thrown forward, making the stance awkward.

THE MECHANICAL "V"

This device allows two shots to be made, and is used when you will have to over-reach and put yourself out of balance to make a shot. Played flat, it enables you to make a normal shot to target center or below center of the cue ball. Turn the high "V" on its side and you can target at a more acute angle for greater effect. Remember when you use this device, always place it gently in position and do not drag it. Move it out of play immediately after you make the shot.

Extending your cue ball control

The match play exercises you have been playing are all designed to improve your appreciation of striking the object ball to pocket it or move it into another position. You will also have begun to feel the pace required to play the cue ball to achieve a given shot. The position the cue ball ends up in is another matter, and this section is about gaining position following a shot.

When playing a natural shot to the pocket, the cue ball has a habit of following the on-ball in!

The mechanical "V" can make life easier in terms of balance, but it loses the feel of the cue.

Your cuing action determines the direction of the cue ball, and your appreciation of pace, how far the cue ball will travel on that line. This accuracy is often not enough. To redress this fault you must learn English and draw.

The challenge of English and draw

Applying English or draw to the cue ball is vital to gain position following any shot. It is not enough to rely on straight or angle shots to win a game. Whether you add English or draw to a shot will affect the result of the collision between the cue and the on-ball. Accurately applied, it can place the cue ball in a more advantageous position for the next shot.

English or draw is applied when the cue strikes the cue ball anywhere other than dead-center to the line of play. Using English or draw and controlling them gives class to your match play, and will earn envy from your opponent.

English and draw are simple names for a fairly complex system of targeting the cue ball to make the ball spin on its base point, and achieve a given direction after it has impacted with the object ball.

The older word for English is side-spin. Draw is back-spin. If you imagine a line drawn through the middle of the cue ball level with the table, the simplicity of the older terms become clear. If you play the ball on the center line, above the middle line, you add top-spin, play the ball on the middle line either left or right of the center line and you add side-spin; play the ball below the middle line and you add back-spin.

The illustrations make the next section easier. Each of the marks are called targets and are arranged quite simply.

The center of the ball is the dead-center, used in all natural shots. If you target the ball on any other mark it will add a bias to the ball. The inner ring shows the approximate positions to target for

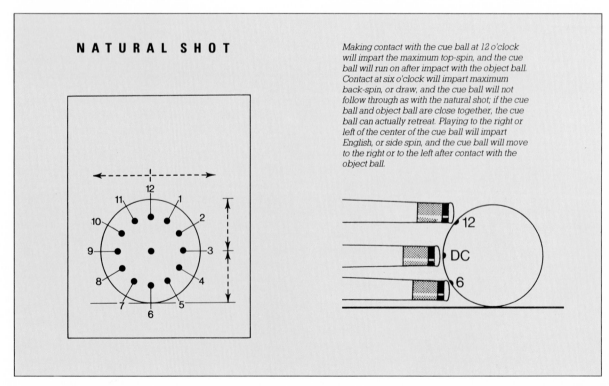

NATURAL SHOT

Making contact with the cue ball at 12 o'clock will impart the maximum top-spin, and the cue ball will run on after impact with the object ball. Contact at six o'clock will impart maximum back-spin, or draw, and the cue ball will not follow through as with the natural shot; if the cue ball and object ball are close together, the cue ball can actually retreat. Playing to the right or left of the center of the cue ball will impart English, or side spin, and the cue ball will move to the right or to the left after contact with the object ball.

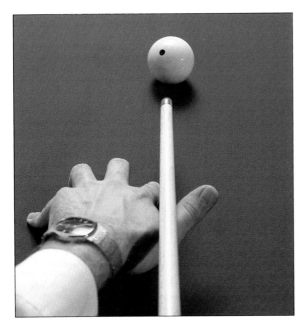

Left-hand English with top-spin, with the bridge slightly raised.

Left-hand English with draw; lower your bridge, do not alter your stance.

normal top-spin, side-spin and back-spin. The outer ring show again approximately where you can safely target to achieve extremes of any of the spins described.

The targets (at 45 degree segments) will give right-hand top-spin (r/h top-spin), left hand back-spin (l/h back-spin) and so on.

Do not let these technical expressions confuse your understanding. They simply show how to add draw and English to your cue ball control.

Adjust your cue action when adding English and draw. The forward swing will be a little heavier than normal. The cue tip will be traveling at its maximum power on impact and it must be smooth and follow through as you have learned. If you try to stop your cue action at the point of impact, you can add unnecessary power to your swing and can cause the cue ball to behave as though it has a mind of its own, often leaping off the table in disgust!

When you play to add English or draw to the cue ball, remember never alter your stance to aim your cue action. Instead *raise* or *lower* your bridge. (There are occasions when it may be necessary to

alter your stance and this is dealt with in later sections.)

THE SIMPLER SHOTS

The basic steps in learning to add English and draw are best kept to natural shots. With practice you will learn just how much extra power you should add to your forward swing to achieve a desired result. Only when you have fully appreciated this new skill will your angle shots benefit.

Top-spin is used when you want the cue ball to overrun the point of contact with the object ball. Obviously, never use it when potting a natural shot.

Practice the action in a natural shot down the table. Don't target too high on the cue ball because this leads to a miscue. Play to keep both balls in a straight line.

Back-spin The effect of back-spin is to reduce the natural follow through when the cue ball strikes the object ball.

Back-spin is best seen when the balls are closer together. Place the cue ball about 15 inches

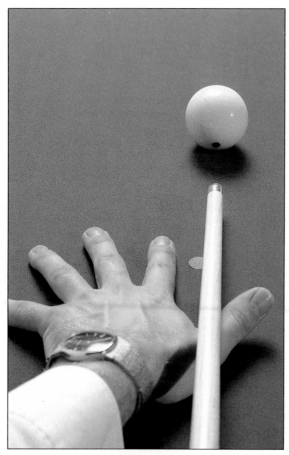

Straight draw shot without English, with a low bridge.

and line up the cue ball about 15 inches away. Use back-spin to its best effect.

As you become familiar with the effects of the simple English and draw, combine them with pace and practice straight and angle shots to gain position following impact.

Spot the cue ball and place the object ball 3 inches from the left-center pocket. Play to pocket and position on the foot spot. Medium-pace, target r/h side-spin to impact ½-ball. Simple isn't it!

Spot the cue ball and place the object ball on the foot spot and play to pocket the object ball in the right-bottom pocket, the cue ball to hit the foot bank and return to near the foot spot. Moderate-pace, aim to the left of the object ball to impact ¼-ball, target r/h top-spin. A slightly more difficult shot but one well worth perfecting.

Apply each practice shot to either side of the table and begin to develop your own practice shots. The more difficult shots will be the ones you probably leave out – an understandable but in-admissible weakness. No game of pool is ever easy. A difficult shot played successfully will often make the rest of the game plain sailing.

To pocket bottom right, ¼-face impact, right-hand top-spin, bringing the cue ball back off the foot bank to the foot spot.

ADDING ENGLISH AND DRAW TO THE BANK SHOT

When you add side English or draw to your shots, the rebound will be different and difficult to control.

from the object ball, and play the shot. As you move the balls further apart you will see the effect of the back-spin draw is dramatically reduced: The further apart the balls are the greater power you must add.

Play down the table with medium-pace and target no lower than the normal spot when you first play this shot. As you become familiar with the shot, increase the power of your swing, and play to keep both balls in a straight line.

The lower you target the cue ball, the greater the effect of the back-spin will be. Low targets, however, are best left until you have full control of your cue and cue action.

Back-spin is especially useful to pot from a natural shot. Place the object ball near a pocket

To pocket center left, ½-face impact, right-hand English, leaving the cue ball around the foot spot.

English to the bank Play across the table on the head string. Medium pace, r/h spin. The cue ball will rebound off the bank to the right of the line of play: The angle of rebound will increase as your target becomes finer.

Play an angled shot with the same stroke: The angle of rebound will be greater and will increase as you target finer.

Play the angle shot again but this time with the opposite target. If you are playing down and across the table and add l/h side-spin, the angle of rebound will decrease. Again the angle will de-crease more as you target finer. You should be able to make the cue ball rebound at 90 degrees to the bank from an angle shot.

Draw to the bank Play again across the head string. Light-pace, low target, natural shot: The draw will reduce the effect of the rebound. It is rare to use draw when making a bank shot, and very difficult to control when you make it. Play an angle shot down and across the table. Use moderate-pace, target low r/h: The ball should rebound and stop before the expected pace length.

● *EXERCISE 17* ●
RIGHT-HAND ENGLISH
OFF THE BANK

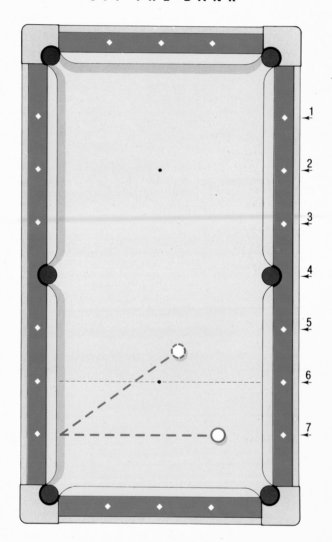

*Played with medium pace and right-hand spin; play
directly across the table. In order to get used to the
effect of English, try to play the cue ball from the
position indicated toward the center pocket.*

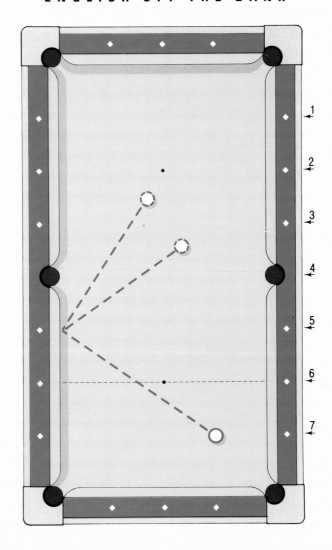

*Obviously, if the cue ball is played with right-hand spin
down the table from left to right at an angle to the bank,
the angle of rebound is increased. Once again, in order
to familiarize yourself with the effects of side-spin, use
some part of the table as an aiming marker: the foot
spot, or the bottom right-hand pocket. If you don't do
this, then the exercise can become redundant, as you
repeatedly spin the ball into the bank without
concentrating upon the actual result of different pace.*

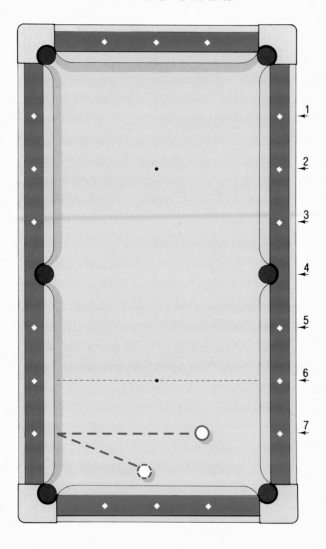

Remember that you are concentrating solely upon side-spin in these exercises – that is, contact with the cue ball at 3 and 9 o'clock – and not on draw or top-spin. Use the center of the head bank as an aiming marker.

● *EXERCISE 20* ●
LEFT-HAND ANGLED
ENGLISH OFF THE BANK

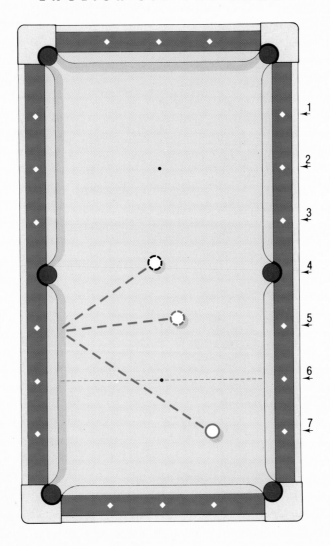

*The angle of return is reduced when the ball is played
down the bank from left to right. Reverse exercises 18
and 20 by playing from the foot of the table against the
same left-hand banks, in order to ascertain if you have
any tendency to play either right-hand or left-hand spin
with greater force or effect.*

THE EFFECT OF THE NAP

When you play a ball the movement will cause friction as it moves over the cloth. The amount of friction will increase when the cloth has a nap, found on all cloths woven from natural fibers. Cloths woven from man-made materials do not have nap.

The nap is the protruding weave on the surface of the cloth. It is usual to determine the condition and direction of the nap before you play on a table. This simple exercise will take a few seconds and is worth remembering.

The nap will run down the table from the head to the foot. Place your hand flat on the table and move it down the table: The nap should lay flat. Move your hand toward the head and the nap should bristle up. On a new cloth, the nap will be quite apparent but less apparent on cloths worn with use.

Playing with the nap will not affect the pace of the cue ball whether you have played it straight or added spin.

Playing against the nap will affect the pace of the cue ball, especially when the cloth is new. A lightly paced straight ball will come to a stop more quickly; but the greatest effect will be apparent when you add spin: The extra friction will increase the effect of the spin.

Power shots

There are few occasions when power-pace shots are necessary. They lack the finesse of all the shots described in previous sections, relying on a powerful forward swing to produce an extreme spin.

Awkward as they will appear, these shots must be part of your armory. You have to adopt a very odd stance, a difficult bridging position and your cuing action will go against all the lessons learned so far. These shots are fraught with danger, not just to the cloth and table but to your cue as well.

The two shots described in this section are the deep swerve and the masse. They are defensive shots and should be played only when there is no other option available. When all the routes to your object ball, directly or indirectly off the cushions, are blocked. These shots have been developed to resolve such situations and have one major drawback in common: to achieve positions or to pot from them is a matter of luck.

To play either the deep swerve or masse, disregard some of the basic elements of pool play – your stance, grip and cuing action.

Not to play them, give the match position, can result in a foul shot being given against you or, in some cases, the match being awarded to your opponent because you have played a deliberate foul.

The deep swerve and masse shots take nerve and concentration. Even though they are rarely played, you must be cue-perfect in their execution.

DEEP SWERVE

The action of a deep swerve shot is to curve the line of play of the cue ball. This is effected by selecting a target spot at the base of the ball, either left or right of the center line, and playing a stab shot with some force at an angle of about 45 degrees from level.

Bridge for right-hand swerve, with the cue held at approximately 45 degrees from the table.

Deep swerve in action; do not let the cuing arm move out from the body in the back swing.

Place the cue ball on the table and take your normal stance. Raise your cue out of parallel to the table, at an angle of about 45 degrees, by bending your right foot until your weight is taken on the ball of the foot. Make a high bridge with your hand, your fingers only touching the cloth. As you swing your cue back you will feel your shoulder muscles tighten. The tendency at this point will be to allow your arm to swing out, but keep your arm tight to your body. As the target spot is low and off center it is vital your aim is steady. As you swing back, you will feel your balance pushed forward unto your bridge hand. Your stance can move out of balance if you delay the shot too long.

The forward swing must be a powerful stab shot, with the action stopping the instant the cue strikes the ball. You can help control the forward swing by tightening your grip.

● *EXERCISE 21* ●
DEEP SWERVE

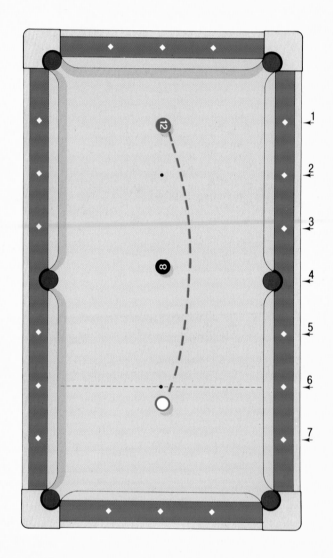

Practice both left- and right-hand deep swerve. Control of the cue ball or the object ball after impact is almost impossible: the aim is simply to get out of trouble.

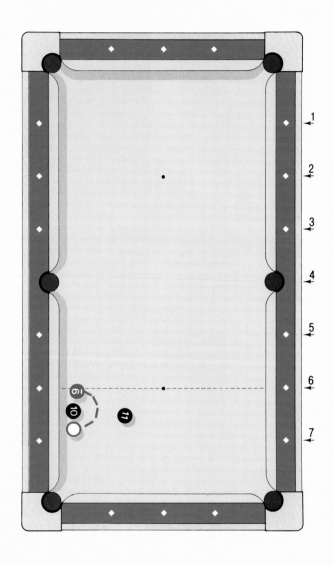

*Desperation time; do not practice this shot to begin with
– on your own table or anyone else's – without first
protecting the cloth with some card. Depending on
local rules, not to attempt this shot may mean that you
forfeit the game. If correctly struck, the cue ball will
move backward slightly on impact.*

Begin your practice with the cue ball and use only moderate force at first. When you are confident you can keep a steady aim and stop the cue on impact, increase the power of your forward swing and begin to swerve the shot.

With practice you will be able to control the swerve of the ball by adjusting both pace and the target spot. As your confidence builds and you have control over the deep swerve, place another ball on the table and play to swerve the cue ball past it to strike a third ball, your object ball. The setup shown will highlight any errors in your appreciation of deep swerve because if the cue ball hits the central ball, it will move and pot the 8-ball!

The object of the deep swerve is to hit your object ball. To achieve anything beyond this is a matter of chance. The deep swerve shot is a defensive shot . . . nothing more.

THE MASSE

To force your opponent into taking the masse shot will give you much pleasure; to be placed into the same situation is to risk losing the game. Where the only route to your object ball is by traveling 180 degrees in a tight circle around the intervening ball and you elect for anything but the masse, many rules will give the game to your opponent because you have played a deliberate foul shot.

The masse shot is similar to the deep swerve but played with cue held at an upright angle, the aim of the cue directly onto the cue ball. The effect is to add massive side spin to the cue ball to pass it around an intervening ball and hit your object ball.

Put a layer or two of cardboard over the table until you can fully control the downward cuing action, preventing damage to the cloth, table bed and your cue tip.

Stand close to the table, move your right leg back and bend the foot. Keep your left leg straight to take your weight. The bridging is just as awkward. Lean slightly forward over the table. Keep

your bridging arm straight, face the palm of your hand away from the table and extend your fingers and form a triangular support with three fingers. Use your little finger to add support to the bridge. You will not be able to easily form the "V" with your thumb, so the cue must be guided down the joint of the first finger and thumb.

Target a spot on the extreme edge of the cue ball. Grip your cue tightly and raise the cue almost upright to the table. If the grip is too uncomfortable, use a lower position. When you make the back swing your arm will tend to move out, so control this as much as you can. Rotating your wrist can sometimes help.

Your downward swing will be a stabbing action and it must be powerful enough to give the cue ball the extreme spin it needs to effect the shot.

The ball will move slightly back on impact, and, as the spin takes over, it will move in a tight circle due to the effect of a top-side spin.

Practice to play around the intervening ball to strike your object ball. The most you can expect from this extremely difficult defensive shot is to hit your object ball . . . to gain position from it would be to expect too much.

When you are play perfect with the masse, remove the protective card. Keep it there until you are!

Note how the little finger is used to attempt to steady the "bridge" for the masse shot. Obviously, almost any shot off the banks is preferable. If the cuing arm feels too uncomfortabe, it may help to take the grip down the shaft.

Game practice

Stance, cue action, pace, angles, bank play, English, draw: now you are ready for game practice.

What are the options? 15 in the center pocket, with enough pace and a touch of left-hand spin to bring the cue ball back for the three, looks good.

Selecting a shot

When the pyramid is split after the opening break, the balls will be spread across the table indiscriminately, and the way you have played the cue ball will determine the next phase of your innings. There will be numerous possibilities, and the problem will be which one to take. Making the shot will be simple enough (after all the practice you have had!); selecting the shot will be a different matter.

Before you continue with, or begin a new innings, take a few seconds and consider the state of the game. Walk around the table and see how the balls lay. Look through the various lines of play open to you, and at the possible pocket shots. View each possibility and plan position for the next shot . . . and the shot after that. If there is no direct line of play, look again. Perhaps there is a plant hiding away almost unseen that, if played in conjunction with a controlled bank shot, would resolve the situation.

So far *Shoot Pool* has dealt only with making

*How about green in the corner pocket, moderate pace,
¾-face natural shot to come back off the side bank for
the five into the middle? (Assuming 8-ball of course).*

shots and the cue control to play them accurately.
The next sections teach how to pocket with a plant,
double off the bank and even make a shot to
nothing and end up with something!

Lining up the shot

Before you play any shot, consider the effect it will
have and the position you want the cue ball to be
for the next shot. Never launch yourself at the
most obvious shot. A better shot might be waiting

to be taken that at first looks a little difficult, but
once taken will produce a very high run.

Look down the line of play to the object ball and
back again to the cue ball. Note how close the
opposing balls lay and any possible hazards. If the
shot is difficult, work out the odds of it being successful. Never play with odds of 100 against; 10 to
1 maybe. When you play the shot, use all the skills
you have to make it count . . . anything less and it
will count against you. Most shots will be natural
shots to the pocket but there are some requiring a
little more consideration to play.

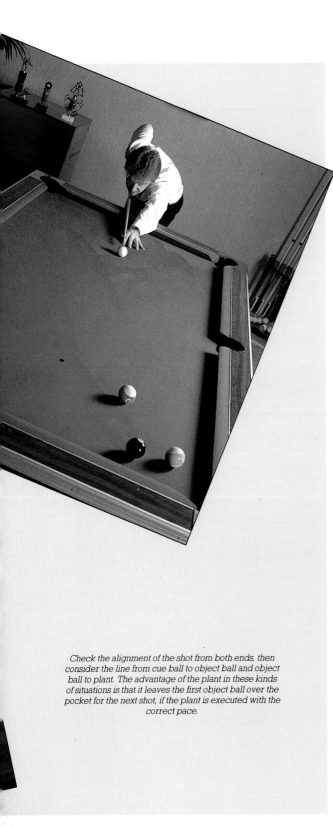

Check the alignment of the shot from both ends, then consider the line from cue ball to object ball and object ball to plant. The advantage of the plant in these kinds of situations is that it leaves the first object ball over the pocket for the next shot, if the plant is executed with the correct pace.

Discovering and playing a plant

A plant is where you play one object ball to another in order to reposition or pocket the second ball. To identify the plant and play it is simplicity itself.

Consider the plant to pocket. Two object balls must align to the pocket. Check the alignment from both angles; the line of play to the pocket and the line of play from the pocket. Once you are certain the plant is on, check the line of play from the cue ball to the first object ball. You should be able to see the object ball full-face or the pot may not be impossible. If not, check the angle shot required to produce the result you want.

The first exercise (23) is the easiest of possible plants to play. Set the table as shown in the illustration. Play a natural shot, medium-pace with draw to hit the 13-ball. The 13-ball will move to hit the 9-ball and drive it into the pocket. The 13-ball will be as easy to pocket as well. Play this with medium-pace and English-left. The cue ball will strike the foot bank after impact and move back up the table. Experiment with other plant shots like this and vary the distance from cue ball to object ball and object to object-ball.

The second exercise (24) uses your knowledge of shots from an angle combined with English. Set the play up as shown in the illustration. The object balls line up to the edge of the pocket to add a little extra difficulty to the shot.

Play moderate-pace with slight left right-hand English and strike the 11-ball slightly off full-face to drive it straight to the 8-ball which will pocket. The cue ball will continue to the foot bank and rebound to just below and in line with the foot spot. Play to the 11-ball with medium-pace left-hand English to impact three-quarter face to pocket. The cue ball will return to about 3 inches above the foot spot via the foot bank. Pocket the 6-ball with medium-pace right-hand English and the cue ball will return to about mid-table off the foot bank.

● EXERCISE 23 ●
TWO-BALL PLANT

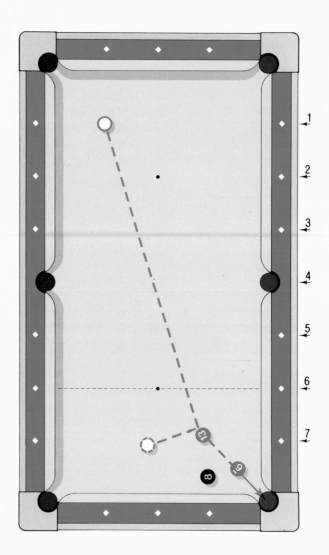

*Draw is an important part of this plant, if the cue ball is
to be conveniently placed for the next shot. Clearly, the
distance from the 13-ball to the 9-ball is very important.
Increase the distance, and any inaccuracy in the shot is
magnified greatly. More than ten inches between the
two object balls and unless you are Jim Rempe, it's
probably not worth the risk.*

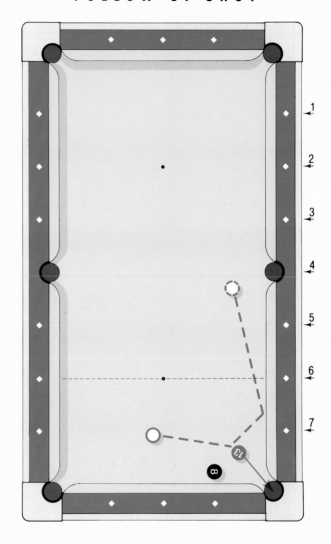

If you do not keep in mind control of the cue ball and the 13-ball when executing the plant, then there is little point in trying it; you could simply pot the 9-ball direct instead. If, however, the advantage of the plant was clear to you and you have used draw, then your next shot should be played medium pace English-left to send the cue ball back up the table.

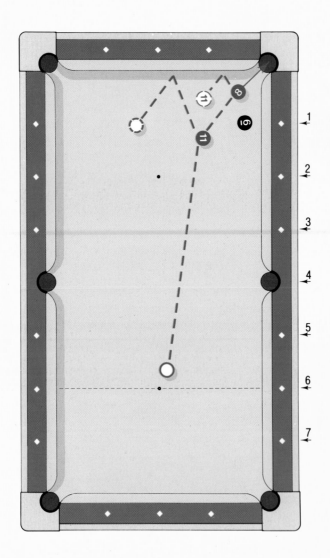

Consider all the angles, and look ahead to the next shot: control the cue ball, and you control the game. 11-ball slightly less than full-face with a touch of English-right to plant the 8-ball, leaving the cue ball below the foot spot.

● *EXERCISE 24A* ●
PLANT WITH ENGLISH –
SECOND SHOT

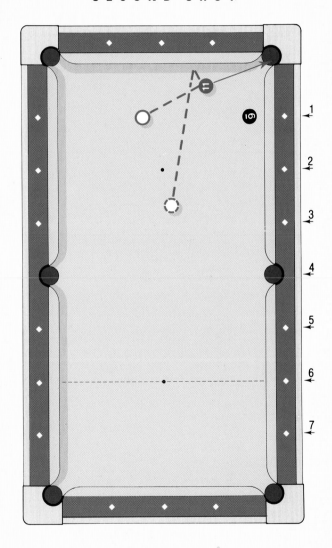

*11-ball in the corner pocket, medium pace, ¾-face,
English-left, to leave the cue ball a little way above the
foot spot, via the foot bank.*

● EXERCISE 24B ●
PLANT WITH ENGLISH –
THIRD SHOT

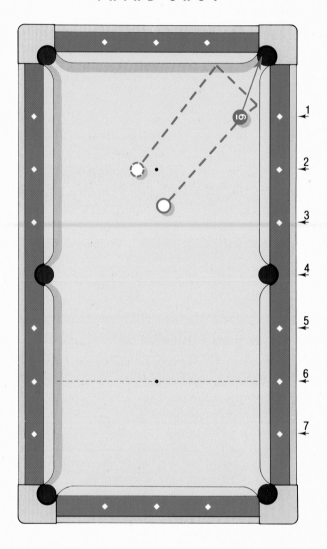

6-ball in the corner pocket, medium pace English-right,
to leave the cue ball about mid-table around the foot
spot; if you succeed with practice sequences like this,
and you don't get much of a kick out of it, you're playing
the wrong game.

Increase the difficulty of this second exercise by including extra balls to complicate the shot. Plant shots are never as easy as the ones shown. The basic ingredient of the plant has to be two balls aligned fairly well to the pocket; never try, unless you are extremely knowledgeable, to pocket a ball using two or more angles . . . that is best left to the master pool shooter. The closer the balls are together the easier the plant shot will be; never attempt it if the object balls are more than 10 inches apart.

The doubled shot

Many players see the doubled shot as a fluke, an accidental but fortunate mistake. This may be the case with the average player, but the skilled player would have deliberately planned and played the shot . . . just another shot from his extensive library!

The doubled shot is taken when the direct line of play to the object ball is obscured by another, and the only option is to use the bank opposite and perhaps the foot bank as well. The doubled shot is both safety and attacking play.

To say the skilled players relish playing the doubled shot is to misunderstand their game. They prefer to see a shot directly through the line of play and only play it when they can be sure of success. After all, they are expected to have a high percentage of their shots producing positive results.

They view the doubled shot with less than the enthusiasm of the novice who, not expecting more than a lucky contact, will jump around with obvious delight when he flukes the ball down the pocket. The doubled shot is always a high-risk shot, and should only be played when all other options are spent . . . and only played with deliberate, calculated care.

You have practiced using the banks and seen the effect of the numerous possibilities open in using them. Use your knowledge to make the following shot:

Place the cue ball to the right of the head spot and the object ball over the center pocket. View the angle from the opposite bank, and stand about mid-way between the balls.

You know the cue ball played with a natural shot will rebound off the bank at the same but opposite angle of impact. Find the apex of this angle and lightly mark this spot on the bank. Play the cue ball direct to this mark and it should rebound, hit and pocket the object ball.

Set the balls up again but move the position of the cue ball 6 inches further down from the head spot. Use the same mark as before and with 1/h-spin play the shot. The spin will reduce the angle of rebound, hit and pocket the object ball. Play these two shots a few times to take the element of luck out of them. If you average six out of 10 you are doing very well – and are well on the way to understanding why the top players avoid them when possible.

All shots are not as easy as the first two practices, so complicate them by adding an extra ball. Play the shot with the cue ball eight inches out from the side bank, one object ball over the right-center pocket and the other ½ inch away up the table. Play to hit the ball over the pocket; hit the other and . . . foul stroke. Use the same setup but play to different pockets and from different angles.

Return to exercise 25 and add an extra dimension of difficulty to the shot. Place the cue and object balls in line with your mark on the opposite bank and play the object ball to the bank to rebound and pocket. Again, add the second ball close to the pocket. If the first object ball pockets the second ball . . . foul stroke again! Expand the practice as before.

You must play these shots again, this time to gain position to pocket the second ball. Using backspin will complicate the shots so concentrate on using side-spin only. Remember, spin will alter the angle of rebound and may be used up after impact with the bank. Again this will depend very much upon the condition of the bank rails.

● *EXERCISE 25* ●
THE DOUBLED SHOT

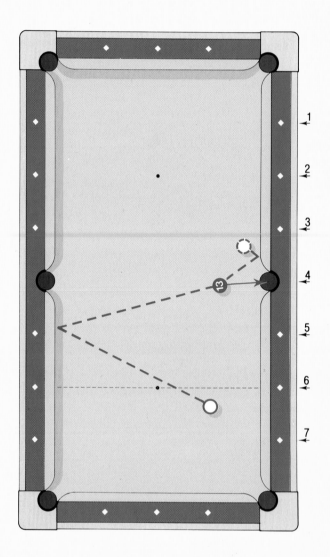

*The doubled shot should be played grudgingly, when
other options are closed, and whenever possible with
safety in mind. Play a natural shot, without English or
draw, using a mark on the side bank equidistant from
the cue ball and the object ball. Medium pace should
see the cue ball come to rest fairly close to the right
bank.*

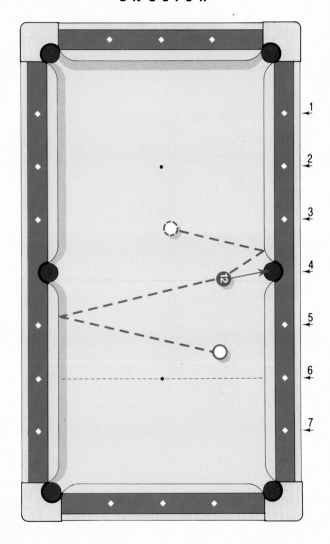

An unpleasant prospect: a doubled shot with English-left. Move the cue ball down the table six inches or so, and using the same mark as before, sink the object ball. Remember that the shot will require more force to initiate the spin, much of which will be absorbed by the bank.

DOUBLED SHOT – WITH
ADDED DISTRACTION

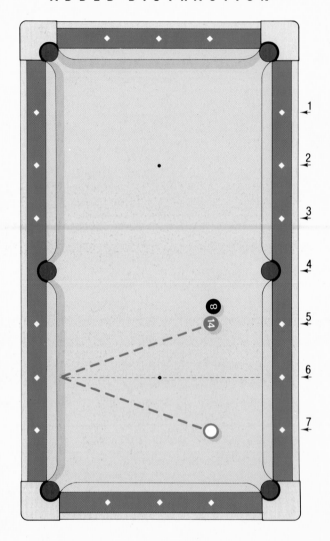

*This is clearly a shot to nothing, an escape act: the
14-ball cannot be potted, and the close proximity of the
8-ball threatens foul shot; so there is no point in trying
anything fancy with English. Play a natural shot, finding
and marking the apex of the triangle on the side bank.*

● EXERCISE 28 ●
DOUBLING THE OBJECT BALL

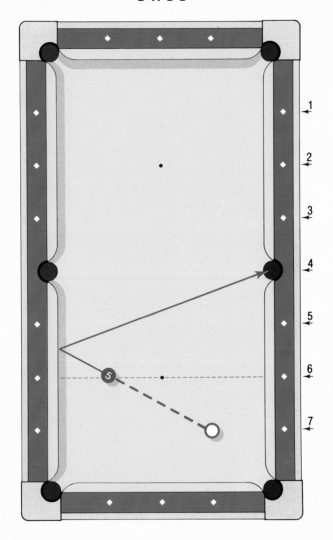

While the lines of impact and angles are more or less the same as in exercise 25, this is in fact probably a more difficult shot to play successfully, because there is more "running time" available to the object ball in which to magnify any inaccuracy after impact with the cue ball, before the pocket is reached. Although obviously, it is easier to make contact with the object ball in the first place, thereby avoiding a foul, and in this sense it is probably a more attractive shot to attempt.

Set the table up again as for exercise 28 but this time place the object ball a little down the table, requiring a three-quarter impact point to pocket. Adjust the mark on the opposite bank to compensate for the change of angle. The objective is to make the cue ball hit the bank and rebound to stop just above the foot spot after impact with the object ball. Increase the shot to between medium- and strong-pace. This shot will need more practice than the first, so play it until you are confident enough to advance to the next phase, using spin. Add a second object ball, this time over the opposite center pocket and use the position gained after the first shot to pocket it, then allow the cue ball to stop near the head spot.

If you are successful, you have just begun to string an innings together!

Banked shots with a difference

These four exercises will add greatly to both your library of shots and give your game an extra sparkle by pocketing the apparently impossible!

Place an object ball about 2 inches out from the left hand bank and 6 inches down from the center pocket. Place the cue ball center table, 12 inches from the center pocket string. Now pocket the cue ball in the right-center pocket!

Play with medium-pace, straight with r/h spin. Target the object ball full face. The shot will make the object ball hit and rebound off the left bank at an angle to pocket in the right-center pocket. The cue ball will veer right from impact, strike the bank and angle off to stop beyond the foot spot. When you have succeeded with the pocket shot, play it from the other side of the table. Increase the difficulty of the shot by moving the object ball a little further down the table and the cue ball again further down and closer to the bank. You will be cuing off the bank rails, so remember the practice you have had to overcome this difficulty.

The next two shots are almost shots to nothing . . . almost. Place the object ball 2 inches off the left cushion and the cue ball 12 inches out from the same bank, on the head string. Play with moderate-pace and medium r/h spin. Target the object ball ¾-face and play the shot. The object ball will hit the bank at an angle and cross the table to pocket. The cue ball will travel down the table and the remaining spin will reduce the angle of rebound from the foot bank to return the cue ball back almost level with the foot spot. This is no shot for the nervous player. Make sure that your aim is steady and accurate. Play it from both sides of the table. This is no trick shot. The skill it takes to play will amaze lesser players than yourself. Play it only when the occasion demands.

The same principle applies to this next shot, and it will take yet more nerve and skill to play. Place the object ball 2 inches out from the left bank, about mid-way between the center and foot pockets. Play the cue ball from the head spot. The goal is to pocket the object ball in the right-foot pocket! Play moderate-pace with r/h spin. Target the object ball ¾-face and play. The object ball will move left on impact, hit the cushion and pocket in the right-foot pocket. The cue ball will travel to the foot bank and the remaining spin reduce the angle of rebound to move the cue ball straight back up the table. To get position following this shot can be very difficult. That's why it is called a shot to nothing . . . almost!

ANGLED DOUBLE

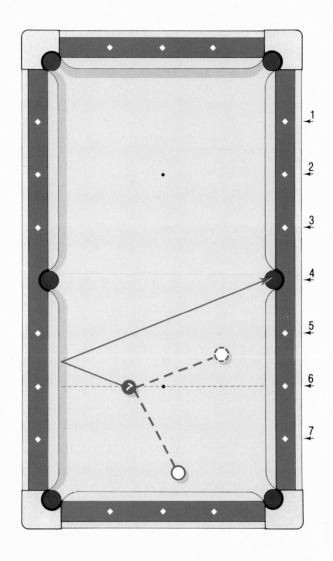

*Move the object ball down the table to demand a
¾-face impact to double and sink the object ball. Adjust
your mark on the rail by trial and error. You think this is
difficult? You're still using natural shots!*

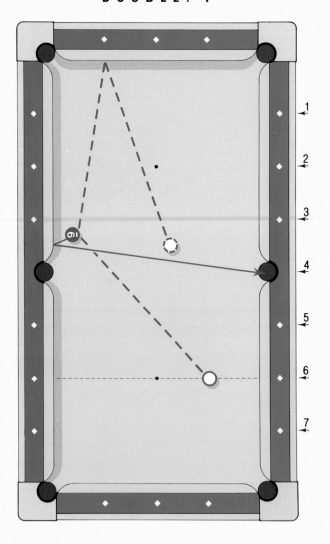

Medium pace, full-face contact with English-right, for the center pocket. When should you attempt such a shot? That of course depends upon the state of the game; if the object ball was the last on the table, and sinking it meant a win for either player, then a safety shot might be preferable, taking the 9-ball down against the center of the foot bank and leaving the cue ball against the side rail, or bringing it back up the table. So much depends upon how you feel about your game at that moment.

● *EXERCISE 31* ●
MATCH-WINNER
DOUBLE : 2

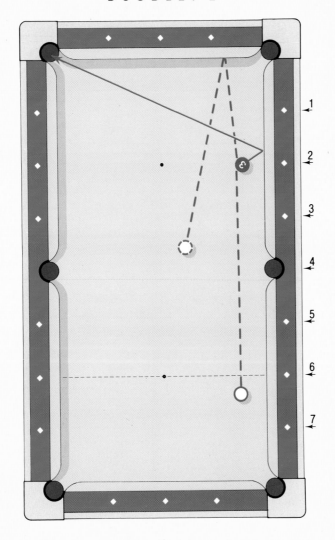

An even harder proposition – but by no means a trick shot: moderate pace, ¾-face impact, English-right. The same bases for deciding on attempting this shot apply as for exercise 30; except that this is probably an even more difficult feat because of the greater distance from cue ball to object ball.

SAFETY PLAY

If you find during your innings that to pocket the next object ball will leave you with no direct line of play, make the next shot to safety. This is perhaps easier said than done but it is essential you never leave the game open.

The objective of a shot to safety is to leave the cue ball in a position that will change your opponent's innings into a nightmare! By positioning the cue ball in the angle trap, forcing a masse or swerve, freezing it against an object ball, safety play will give your opponent the most impossible of bridges, angles, back-spin and side-spin. It is designed to make him foul stroke . . . and give you "ball-in-hand."

Too much safety play can ruin a game of pool. Pool is a dynamic game; a game of pocketing with skill and high runs. Keep it that way. Calculated safety play will add gamesmanship to your play and carefully layed-on it can drive your opponent off the rails. That is unless he turns the table on you!

A typical situation where safety play can be used is shown in the diagram:

The game is rotation and it is your innings. The 8-ball has just been pocketed and the 9-ball is on. The problem is if you pocket the ball, how do you get position for the 10-ball? Leaving that to your opponent is the best strategy.

The objective is to play the cue ball medium-pace with l/h-spin to impact the 9-ball ¼-face to the left bank, rebound with l/h-spin and move down toward the foot bank. Set the table up as shown and play this dreadful safety shot . . . then play your opponent's innings!

Try this shot. Play a natural ball, moderate-pace to the right hand bank about 5 inches down from the head string. The ball should rebound to the head bank, off that to the left hand bank and, hopefully impact the 9-ball . . . miss, and foul stroke, ball-in-hand.

The game is 14.1 and it is your innings. The 9-ball pocket is a natural but there is nothing on

beyond that. You can play a fine-cut on the 8-ball but this will disturb the cluster. Play with light-pace, deep r/h back-spin to impact the 9-ball ¾-face. The 9-ball will move sharply left hit the cushion and move behind the cluster, the cue-ball moves right after impact, hit the foot bank and angles away to stop almost where it began its journey. There is nothing on for your opponent except misery . . . so play his innings!

Play this shot. All that is visible is the 8-ball full-face, ¾-face of the 7-ball and just more of the 4-ball. Play a natural shot moderate-pace with deep back-spin to impact the 4-ball full face. The cue ball should stop (perhaps just on the bank), the object ball rebounding off the bank to stop just on or beyond the left side bank around the head string.

When you have played into and out of these two set pieces, you will see just how awkward a position your opponent can be left after considered safety play. Other occasions will require use of the masse or deep swerve. You must recognize these situations as they occur.

Jean Balukas, one of the most successful players on the women's circuit today.

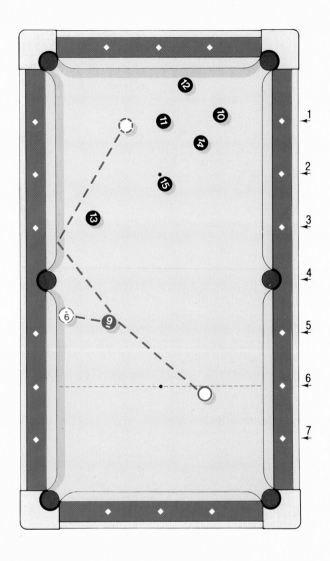

*Remember: control the cue ball and you control the
game. It is not always the best policy to go for your
shots, as in this case, with access to the 10-ball blocked.
Play medium pace, ¼-face impact, English-left, to leave
the 9-ball against the side bank and the cue ball behind
the 13-ball – or better still – behind the 11-ball.*

● EXERCISE 32A ●
SAFETY PLAY ESCAPE

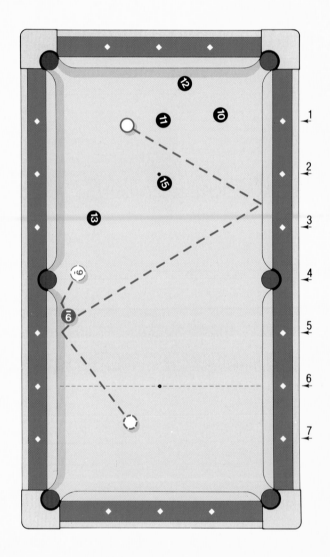

*Play your opponent's shot to escape from the position
set up by the exercise on the previous page: a natural
shot off the right bank. Because these kinds of shots are
difficult enough without any further complication, and
are merely attempts to avoid a foul, always play a
natural shot whenever possible, without spin, aiming to
strike the object ball in the center.*

How to pocket the four balls in order from this position? A classic test of control of the cue ball and of strategy.

Further practice sessions

THE FOUR SPOT ANGLE SPREAD

When you have conquered the simple angle shot exercises, try this long shot to pocket from four different angles. The photograph foreshortens the actual length of the table and makes the shots look simple. We have used, from left to right, the 8-ball, 9-ball, 5-ball and 3-ball. Pocket them in order from 8 through 3. If you miss a ball, keep playing it until you pocket it in the correct pocket . . . with all the others in the left-foot pocket! Try to bring the cue ball back to the same spot after each shot. Your appreciation of side-spin, angle and straight shooting will be put to the test . . . as will your patience! The shot sequence – pace, spin, angle and bank – will be found at the end of the Match Play chapter. Only look there if you really cannot work out the sequence for yourself. This is the real skill of pool play.

THE FIVE-IN-LINE HIGH RUN

Part of every top player's warm up session is a practice similar to the five-in-line high run session. It comprises pocketing exercises combined with natural, angle, draw and English shots. The practice is played through until all balls are in the pocket. Not one here and another some time later, but in one high run. Whenever the innings is over (failure to pocket), the balls are reset in their original positions and the practice begins over again.

The practice also includes positional shots from both straight and bank shots. So, look out for the deliberate traps!

Use any object balls you choose: we have played (from the foot bank upward) 12-ball, 11-ball, 8-ball, 9-ball and 13-ball. There is no need to evenly space them apart but they should be more or less in line. Play the cue ball from the head string to rebound (or better still stop) on the foot string line. (Highlight 1: medium-pace)

Pocket the 12-ball and move the cue ball off the r/h bank. (Highlight 2: light-pace, fine r/h-spin)

Pocket the 9-ball and stop short of the l/h-center pocket. (Highlight 3: light pace, low back-spin)

Pocket the 11-ball and position the cue ball close to the l/h foot pocket. (Highlight 4: light-pace, fine l/h-spin)

Pocket the 13-ball and position the cue ball below the l/h center pocket via the right side and head banks. (Highlight 5: strong-pace, r/h-spin and fine cut)

Pocket the 8-ball and leave the cue ball on the foot spot. (Highlight 6: medium-pace stun shot to full face)

Playing time about 5 minutes maximum.

If you want to increase the difficulty of the five-in-line high run exercise, try playing it in the reverse order!

FIVE-IN-LINE: THE PROFESSIONAL'S PRACTICE SESSION

Shots to impress

There is no better way to dominate a match than to close it with an absolutely devastating shot . . . and then play it again just to show off your prowess.

The shots that follow are by no means easy as you will have seen from your practices on doubled shots with a difference. They all require concentration and a great deal of skill to play successfully. When you see the opportunity to play them, don't get over-excited and take your time. A sudden burst of adrenalin can convert the shots into total disaster. Each shot is a test of your appreciation of the single, double and treble banked shot, draw and English, target and impact shots.

THE TREBLE COCKED HAT

The objective is to play the object ball off three cushions to end up in the center pocket. The difficulty lies in the closeness of the object ball to the bank. Miss the pocket and you can claim a shot played to safety.

Position the balls as shown and play a medium-pace, right hand-spin. Play a natural shot; the object ball will rebound off the right bank, on to the left of the foot bank and drop obediently into the opposite center pocket. The cue ball will move into the head area and stop close to the head bank. Should the object ball miss the pocket, it will travel down the table and stop on the foot bank . . . a very clever safety shot (you can claim).

THE FIVE BANK POWER FINALE

This shot will add a brilliant finish to any match. Played off five banks with a careless-looking power pace this *coup de grâce* is certainly the master players' stroke.

The obvious option is to play the object ball, medium-pace targeted about ¼-face. But why play such a simple shot?

● *EXERCISE 33* ●
THE TREBLE COCKED HAT

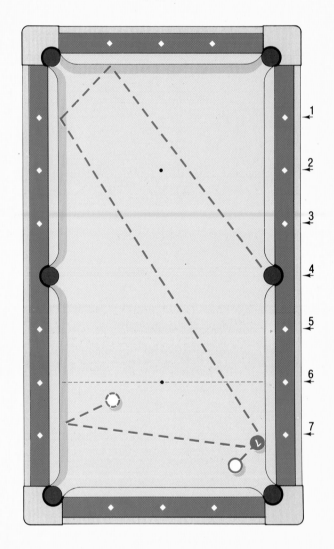

There is little point in not playing pool to win: but there will be occasions in friendly games when you can attempt difficult shots like this just for the fun of it, and for the immense satisfaction to be gained if they come off. Quite heavy English-right is required for this shot.

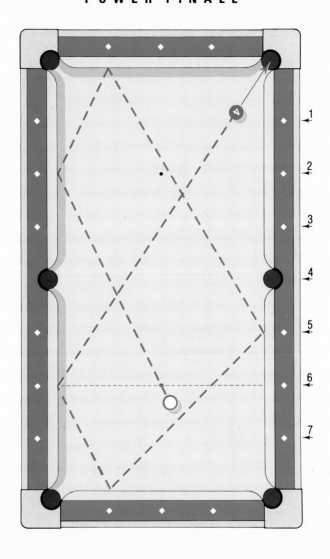

*When practicing, this shot is an excellent reminder of
the basic angles represented by the diamond grid;
when playing, it's a scene-stealer – and will certainly
give you the psychological edge for the next game!*

Play a power shot, first to the right bank on the 6-string line. The ball will carry to the head bank, the left bank, the foot bank, the right bank, finally impacting the object ball with just enough pace to pocket it into the top-left pocket.

If your accuracy is less than perfect, the shot will look like an amateur's and the mistake will leave you open to the derision of any spectators around. But if it comes off! You'll feel on top of the world.

THE SIMPLE COCKED HAT

If the treble looks difficult, try the "simple" version. Position the balls as shown. Play the shot with right hand-spin at medium-pace. The object ball will rebound off the foot rail and drop into the center pocket. As with the treble version, a miss can be claimed as a safety shot! If the object ball fails to pocket, it will travel up the table and stop by the head bank. Meanwhile, the cue ball will rebound and stop by the left bank. If you use draw with this shot, the cue ball will actually stop close to the foot bank, adding an extra edge to the "safety" aspect of the shot.

HIGH RISK DOUBLE SHOTS

The accuracy needed to play these shots will place you in the master-player class. There is no safety aspect with either of these shots, and a miss can pass the game to your opponent. These shots require a fine appreciation of pace as well. A miss will place the object ball close to the pocket and the cue ball easily positioned to pocket. Played well and accurately, they will completely overawe your opponent.

Played to the center pocket Position the balls as shown. Play a medium-pace shot, targeted straight to impact the object ball ¼-face. The object ball will hit the left bank and rebound into the opposite center pocket. Miss, and the object ball will stop close to the pocket, leaving your opponent a simple shot to pocket. If you feel that this is too simple,

place a second object ball to the left of the on-ball and slightly off line. When you can master this little extra difficulty, the shot will surely impress.

Played off the foot bank This shot is a further extension of the previous one and will certainly draw a stunned admiration from your opponent . . . or a look of pure happiness from your opponent if you fail.

Play a natural shot with moderate-pace to impact the object ball ¼-face. The resulting collision will drive the object ball to rebound off the right bank and speed into the left foot pocket. The cue ball will travel up the table to stop about the 4-string line. A miss will leave the object ball an easy target to pocket. There is no safety aspect in this shot.

Another great player of recent times, as pictured by Dan and Tom Birkbeck. Ray Martin holds a high run of 382 balls.

THE SIMPLE COCKED HAT

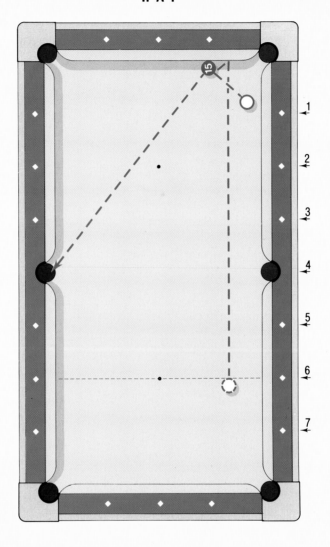

This is actually a fairly safe shot to attempt, because if you miss, the cue ball and object ball are far apart, and the cue ball is left inconveniently tucked up against the side bank, or with draw, the foot rail. Play with medium pace, English-right.

Game play

Selecting a shot, the plant, doubled shots, safety play, advanced practice sessions: you are now ready to take on the world.

Basic pool rules

Before you play any serious match make sure you know the full house or tournament rules. You cannot claim lack of knowledge if a decision or shot goes against you and hope that you will be forgiven your error. Pool is too serious for that!

There are some rules that never vary; rules that are so obvious that they are rarely written – rules that you should never forget. Some players call them etiquette, others just common sense.

◊ Never obstruct your opponent's game. Stand back from the table and leave your comments until his innings is over. Some house rules will actually award the game to your opponent is you cause him to miscue or foul stroke.

◊ Never deliberately play out of turn.

◊ Never play a shot when the cue ball or any other ball is in motion. Again, some house rules will award the game to your opponent.

◊ Never smoke over the table or leave your drink balanced on the rails. If you spin a coin to decide the first break, spin the coin away from the table.

FOUL STROKE

Of the numerous rules that pool is structured by, none are as complicated as those that describe the foul shot. For the purposes of *Shoot Pool* only those rules that help your practice are described. They may not be the actual rules that are played locally, but they should be observed in your training sessions. The basic term the "on-ball" is the object ball that you nominate to play. The foul stroke is committed when a player:

◊ Plays to any other object ball other than the on-ball.

◊ Pockets directly any other object ball other than the on-ball. (This rule – and others – can depend upon the type of pool being played.)

◊ Plays directly on to an object ball and not the cue ball.

◊ Pockets the cue ball directly or indirectly.

◊ Causes any ball in play to leave the table.

◊ Touches any ball in play, either directly or with any part of his clothing.

◊ Plays the cue ball and fails to impact on the on-ball.

◊ Plays any ball that is in motion.

When a player is awarded a foul stroke his opponent is given the cue ball "in hand." The cue ball is taken from where it lies and repositioned to be played from any point within the head area (between the head string and head bank.) Only one shot is played for the ball-in-hand advantage. When a player plays a foul stroke his innings is over.

Ball off the table This occurs when any ball is played off the table during an innings. The cue ball is given ball in hand to the opposing player. An object ball is positioned on the foot spot or as close as possible to this position along the long line. It must not be re-positioned touching any other ball.

Pocketed balls Any object ball that is pocketed, legally or illegally, remains out of play until the pyramid is re-racked or the game is over. Only the cue ball can be returned to play and is awarded ball in hand to the opposing player.

When one or more object balls are pocketed and the shot is deemed a foul stroke, the total of the numbers on the ball(s) or the total number of balls is added to the point score of the opposing player.

The rules of the following pool games are only given in their basic form, enough for you to understand how the game is played but not enough for you to be able to make a positive decision over the finer points of play.

14.1 CONTINUOUS PLAY

14.1 shares with 8.1 the title as the most popular international pool game. The objective is to play for points and the winner is the first player to reach a given total of points at a certain point in the game (the number is up to you and your opponent to decide upon before starting) or the player who has the greatest number of points after a given number of games.

Arrange the object balls in the pyramid exactly as in the diagram. Place the apex ball on the foot spot and make sure the base of the pyramid is parallel to the foot bank. Players lag for the opening break.

The cue ball is played from anywhere in the head string area. The first player must play directly to the apex ball and split the stack. At least two of the object balls must hit any of the banks or a called ball may be pocketed.

If the player fails to do either or scratches the cue ball, he will have played a foul stroke and the next player is awarded two points. If the cue ball is scratched even though two object balls hit the bank or the called ball is pocketed legally, the opposing player will be awarded one point. When this happens the first player's innings is over.

The next player can then either play the balls as they lay or have the balls re-racked.

The player can call any object ball and play it only to the pocket he nominates.

He can pocket as many balls from the one shot

only if he pockets the object ball as well.

His innings is over when he fails to pocket an object ball, scratches the cue ball, plays to safety or commits a foul stroke.

If a player pockets an object ball directly that has not been called, or plays the called ball to another and pockets it and does not pocket the called ball, the total of the number of balls pocketed is added to the opponent's score. The player has also made a foul stroke.

If an object ball is played off the table it can be repositioned anywhere along the long line on or as near to the foot spot as possible. The face value

Racked in preparation for a game of 14:1 continuous play.

of points is added to the opponent's score. Object balls are never put back on the table after they have been pocketed legally.

If, during an innings only one object ball is left in play and the total number of points has not been reached, the game is temporarily halted. The cue ball and object ball remain in position on the table and the other pocketed balls are re-racked. The position which the last object ball would take in the rack is left blank. The player then commences his innings playing either to the pyramid or the remaining object ball.

The rack for 14:1 rotation pool.

ROTATION POOL

This is another version of playing to score points from the balls pocketed. In rotation, the actual face value of each ball is added to make the total points scored.

The balls can be placed in any order in the pyramid except that the 1-ball is positioned at the apex, the 2-ball at the bottom-left corner and the 3-ball in the bottom-right corner.

The opening break is determined by lagging. The first player plays directly to the apex ball and splits the pack. There is no need for any object ball to hit a bank. If a player scratches the cue ball, the opposing player plays ball-in-hand from the head string area.

When a player begins an innings he must play the balls in ascending order beginning from the 1-ball. His innings is over when he fails to pocket the object ball, scratches the cue ball or makes a foul stroke.

If an object ball leaves the table it is a foul stroke, and the face value of that ball is added to the opposing player's score. The ball is then placed in a pocket and not returned to the table. If the cue ball is scratched, it is played ball-in-hand from the head string area and no extra points are added to the opposing player's score.

The balls are re-racked after each game until one player reaches the total of 61 or whatever other total has been agreed.

Some people call 8-ball the "thinking-man's" game. Not that you will have to plan the game any more than 14.1 or rotation, but the game can sometimes rely on lengthy safety play. Whatever other people's opinion may be, 8-ball is as popular throughout the pool world as 14.1.

Make the pyramid as shown in the illustration, ensuring the balls are placed in alternating order along the sides. It is important to have the 8-ball in the center of the 3rd row behind the apex ball. To win, a player must pocket all the balls in his

The rack for 8-ball.

nominated set (spot or stripe) and finally pocket the 8-ball. The opening break is decided by lagging.

The first player must play directly to the apex ball and at least two object balls must hit any bank. If one object ball pockets from the opening break, this nominates the set he must play. If two or more balls are pocketed, the player can nominate the set he chooses. If only one or no object ball hits the cushions it is a foul stroke, and the next player can play from the position the balls lay or have them re-racked.

If the cue ball is scratched at the opening break, even if two balls have hit the banks or one or more object balls have been pocketed, the player has played a foul stroke. The next player can play ball-in-hand as the other balls lay or have them re-racked. Any balls that have been pocketed remain in the pockets and are not returned to the table.

A player may only pocket balls of his elected set. He may pocket any object ball to any pocket, and there is no need to call or nominate. A player's innings is over when he fails to pocket the object ball, plays to safety, scratches the cue ball or makes a foul stroke.

If a player pockets an opponent's balls directly or indirectly, he has made a foul stroke and the object ball remains in the pocket and is not returned to the table. If a player plays an opponent's ball directly, he has made a foul stroke. If the object ball leaves the table, it is a foul stroke and the object ball will be put in a pocket and not returned to the table. The cue ball, however, is returned to the table and played ball-in-hand from anywhere in the head string area. If the 8-ball leaves the table, it is a foul stroke and the ball is returned to the table on the long line on or as near as possible to the foot spot.

If the 8-ball is pocketed directly or indirectly, the game is over and awarded to the opposing player.

In simple 8-ball you do not need to call a ball or nominate a pocket. When you have pocketed all the balls of your nominated set, then it's necessary to nominate the pocket for the 8-ball and play directly to it. (Whoever called it *simple* 8-ball?)

Eight-ball is the most international of the pool games, and, consequently, the rules vary from one club to the next. Be careful when shooting pool in a new venue to check the house rules first.

9.1

Wherever 9-ball is played you can be sure they play different rules to you. The simple way is always the best or so it may seem. The game is played with 9 balls in play, and no points are needed to win. The winner is the player who

Racked up for 9:1.

pockets the last ball, and that must be the 9-ball.

Make the pyramid with object balls numbered from 1 to 9. They can be placed in any order but the 9-ball must be in the center of the third row, and the 1-ball at the top. The opening break is decided by lagging.

The balls are pocketed in ascending order beginning from the 1-ball.

The first player must play the cue ball to one bank before impacting the pyramid. If an object ball other than the 1-ball is pocketed from the opening break, the player has made a foul stroke and his innings is over. If the first player scratches the cue ball on the opening break, he has played a foul stroke and his innings is over. The next player shoots ball-in-hand from anywhere in the head string area, he may play the balls as they lay after the foul stroke or have them re-racked.

A player can pocket any number of object balls in any one shot as long as the on-ball is pocketed with the same shot. If the on-ball fails to pocket, the player's innings is over.

An innings is over when a player fails to pocket the on-ball, plays to safety or makes a foul stroke.

When a player plays an innings he must call a ball and nominate a pocket. A player may pocket any number of balls in one shot as long as he also pockets the called ball. The innings is over when he fails to pocket a nominated ball, plays to safety or plays a foul stroke.

If an object ball leaves the table it is a foul stroke, and the ball is returned to the table on the long line on or as near as possible to the foot spot.

If an object ball is illegally pocketed it remains in the pocket and will not be returned to the table. The shot is a foul stroke.

If the cue ball leaves the table it is a foul stroke and the next player shoots ball-in-hand from anywhere in the head string area.

The 9-ball is the last ball to be pocketed, and the player who pockets this ball is the winner.

First games

Now is the time to review how well you have learned to shoot pool. No one can expect you to go through the hundreds of practice sessions suggested for cue control and cue ball control without practicing the lessons in a game situation. Novices and aspiring players should play these simple games with someone they can trust. Preferably someone with more game experience and with a calm disposition. Ask him or her to criticize your match play and point out any weaknesses – and don't take offence.

Play whatever pool game you choose: 14.1, 8.1, 9.1 or rotation and play it game for game. If you elect to play 14.1, make the winning number over three games; any longer and any defeat you suffer will be greater! Take your time in choosing a shot, even asking your opponent's opinion. These first games will highlight any faults you may have developed, and it is vital you return to the practice sessions to eliminate them. If you overlook a fault, it will persist and become a major obstacle in your match play development.

Keep the games simple and play within your limitations. If you try shots you have not mastered, failure in these first games may put you off trying for them for ever.

Every player has his favorite way of loosening up before a match and you must develop your own. Even a few days away from the table can reduce your match play potential.

Step 1 Get your cue action working with a few natural shots across and down the table. Play some shots to pocket with a combination of natural and angle. Keep these first few minutes to simple shots.

Step 2 Get your English and draw working. Make sure your back-spins are perfect and you can effect precise side-spin. Play shots to the banks and to single object balls.

Step 3 Get your high-run set-up working. Use the

five-ball line and practice in the way suggested from both sides of the table. If you miss any ball to pocket, set the five up again.

Step 4 Get your game under control. From the three previous steps you will have recognized at least one slight out-of-form problem. Practice to sort it out. If it persists, try to avoid a match play situation where the problem might arise. Never let the problem dominate your game and treat it like a headache . . . a couple of aspirins and it will go away. The aspirin will be your practice sessions after the game.

Step 5 Get yourself under control. Never let your opponent or spectators spoil your game. Silence them with your skills in pool. Make any mistake look like a deliberate trap for your opponent and only apologize when you have won the game with such style and class!

The third player

Whenever you hear another player saying, "I gave the game away," he is really saying he was beaten by himself as well as the other player. He was not prepared to win except by a chance. No matter how long your practice sessions stretch or how comprehensive your understanding of the game, if you are not self-motivated, your chances of winning the match are very slim.

Pool is an extremely competitive sport. Your opponent will leap on your slightest mistake and take obvious delight in exploiting it. How you react to your mistake will dominate your game from this point on. Forget it the moment you have played the shot or else this will side-track you from your play. Leave self-criticism to later. If your opponent mocks your bad shot, shut him up with your next shot, and don't get into a shouting match.

Winning is what pool is about. When you string-off, be prepared to win and never let your opponent's reputation or skills lessen your determination. He is only human after all! If you have gone through your match-ready practices and can summon all

of your match play skills, then winning will be the natural result. If you lose to a better player, the match will have been truly satisfying and another experience to build your confidence. Losing because your play has been upset by your opponent's gamesmanship and your resulting poor play is an experience nobody relishes.

Your self-motivation is simple. Play to win and play with all of the skills you have learned. Be prepared to lose but only to a better player playing with greater skill. Learn from his skills and approach to the game. Pool is a game where you rarely learn from your own mistakes, only regret making them!

The other third player

The third player that no pool match can be without is the referee or umpire. In person or in written words, this arbiter is always present. His rulings govern every game played and to disagree with, or even worse, ignore his direction, is the cause of almost every type of bad behavior seen on today's pool tables.

The rules are the structure the game is played around. For a player to ignore or deliberately misread them will always be a step backward into the dark days when pool was indeed "played by the boys in the back room" with little skill or regulation.

Each pool authority has its set rules, and it is vital you read them and understand them before starting. Whether the rules are nationally accepted or just the house rules, they are the ones you must play to. If your opponent seems to be rather hazy about them or their application to a particular shot, never decide by yourself. Let some other person adjudicate and let his word be final. An argument during a match will destroy your concentration, disrupt the flow of the game and, all too often, leave a bad taste in your mouth.

No one ever wins a match by shouting at the table.

Playing competitive pool

Wherever pool is played, it always draws spectators. As the game grows steadily in popularity the audiences become larger, attracting bigger sponsorship which in turn draws more interest from the media. Coverage of pool tournaments in the US is greater than any other country, drawing thousands of viewers to the cable channels to watch players entertain with amazing shows of skill and potting . . . with the winners taking amazing money prizes.

If you are serious about entering the competitive pool circuit you must be extremely confident in your play and show it in every match; matchplay that dazzles will attract the organizers. Your play must be consistent and high scoring, and your conduct on the table beyond reproach. A skillful amateur player will always attract the attention of his club and the area he plays in. This must be your first goal.

You can only play for a team by invitation and a place on any team is jealously guarded. Once elected to the team your match play must be consistent for you to retain your position. Any lapse

Howard Vickery

Pete Fusco

Nick Varner

Mike Lebron

Jimmy Fusco

Larry Hubbert

Allen Hopkins

Mike Zuglan

Dick Lane

Tom Jennings

Birkbeck
"The Twins"
DEC.88

Dan Birkbeck
Jan. 1985

Best Wishes
Jimmy Caras

Jimmy Caras, five-times world champion (in 1936, 1938, 1939, 1949 and the BCA US open in 1967), still plays exhibition matches today.

and you can be easily relegated to the sidelines. Only when your performance in the club team is consistent can you dream of representing your county or area. Once again, such positions are fought for with great competition. Being an area player does not automatically select you for professional play.

To become a professional player, you must obtain a license. Only when you have impressed a panel of your peers with your standard of play will the license be granted. Then, having a license will not automatically earn you a living. If you fail to catch the eye of the organizers you may have to rely on sponsorship, and sponsorships are hard to come by, especially for the new professional.

When you become a professional pool player, be prepared for some hard lessons. Even though your game is polished, natural and your personality above the normal player, any mistakes you make will be put under a microscope and blown up beyond belief. You must be able to smile when criticism goes beyond the game you play on the table. There is no easy money in pool, only hard-earned dollars.

The life of a top pool player is not all it seems. He or she is expected at all times to be able to keep up a high standard of play, even when mere mortals would prefer to be anywhere but at a pool table. He or she must be able to shoot pool on the worst tables, take on the local hero and win, get off a trans-Atlantic flight and immediately play a match against a player he has never met . . . and be expected to win.

Two great players on today's circuit, and one from a different generation: "Machine Gun" Lou Butera (TOP), Mike Sigel (ABOVE) and Luther Lassiter (LEFT), who, along with Arthur Cranfield Jr., was at the top throughout the 1960s.

The portraits of great players past and present reproduced in this book are by Dan and Tom Birkbeck of Horsham, Pa. (**BELOW**) The Birkbecks are identical twins who have successfully combined their two great loves – art and pool – and can count many of the players they have portrayed as personal friends. (**RIGHT**) Irving Crane, by "the twins."

THE FOUR SPOT ANGLE SPREAD: PAGE 105

The correct method for sinking the four balls as shown on page 105 is easy to describe – but difficult to execute with any degree of consistency. Remember that the aim is not merely to pot the balls, but to return the cue ball to the head spot after each shot.

First pocket the 8-ball: a natural shot played to impact fine cut. Next, the 9-ball: another natural shot, but impact should be about ¾ face. Be careful with the third shot to the 5-ball: this shot aligns cue and object ball to the pocket. Play with slight right-hand spin to impact dead center. The fourth shot to the 3-ball is a real challenge even for the professional: play with left-hand spin to impact dead center, with enough pace to bring the cue ball back to the head spot off two banks.

If these shots begin to get a little too easy, vary the practice in the second, third and fourth shots by playing power pace with deep screw. Target as before, ensuring that the cue ball returns to the head spot each time.

Index

Acknowledgements

The author and publishers would like to thank the
following for the provision of information,
equipment and images:
Archway Pool and Snooker Club; The Billiards
Library, Long Beach, Ca.; Dan and Tom Birkbeck;
Masterplay Promotions Ltd and the British
Association of Pool Table Operators; Parris Cues,
London; Thurston and Co Ltd, London.
Special thanks are also due to Hazel Grove Music,
Manchester, for the loan of tables and equipment
for photography.